# The *REAL BOOK* About
# SPACE TRAVEL

# The REAL BOOK About

# SPACE

Illustrated by CLIFFORD GEARY

GARDEN CITY BOOKS • GARDEN CITY, NEW YORK

# TRAVEL

## by HAL GOODWIN

Edited by Helen Hoke

BY ARRANGEMENT WITH FRANKLIN WATTS, INC.

The illustrations on pages 91 and 140 have been adapted from SPACE MEDICINE, edited by John P. Marbarger, published by the University of Illinois Press, Urbana, Illinois.

# Contents

# Introduction to Space

THE REAL BOOK OF SPACE TRAVEL is about a subject so modern and exciting that it seems like reading science fiction or the comic strips. When you look up at the moon and the stars, the idea of ever reaching them seems more like a dream than anything else.

But space travel is no longer a wild dream, for right now man's first scouts are being built for a journey across the space frontier. And if man can send scout rockets into space, the time is not far off when he will be able to go himself.

This book doesn't say when men will reach space, because no one knows just yet. But it does try to tell how we can reach space, and why.

It is important for young people to understand how and why, because they are the ones who must live in the coming age of space travel. New things and new words must be learned. It would be hard to know how a space rocket would work without first having a clear understanding of what makes a Fourth of July skyrocket work. It would be hard to understand what kind of life we might find on Mars without knowing a little about life here on earth.

The purpose of this book is to help those interested in space travel to understand what they read or see, and to separate truth from fiction. For now that we have reached the age of space travel, we can expect a lot of both.

In writing this book, the author had the help and advice of several friends and associates. They include Dr. Victor Halbmillion, Ernest G. Reuning, Dr. Norvin C. Kiefer, Rear Admiral Garrett P. Schuyler, Dr. H. Kenneth Gayer, and Alan and Gordon Gayer.

However, the opinions and conclusions are entirely the author's, and any Martians or Venusians who object to comments on their planets should complain only to the person responsible.

HAL GOODWIN
*Washington, D. C.*

8

# 1

# The New Frontier

One by one the frontiers of earth have been crossed. Explorers and adventurers have traveled almost everywhere on earth, until it is hard to find a place where no man has ever been.

There is still much we don't know about our own planet. But so many frontiers have been crossed that adventurers who like to blaze trails must look beyond the earth for a new challenge. Today the trail blazers look upward to the stars.

## SPACE

That is what the doorway to the stars is called. Space has always been there, beyond earth's atmosphere. There was space before there was an earth or a sun. But today we look toward space because what men have dreamed for centuries is becoming real. Now, men say, this greatest of all frontiers can be crossed.

No matter what you like to read—or if you listen to radio or watch television—you are apt to find tales of space. There are stories of spacemen, of travel between the planets or between the stars, of exploration on strange worlds in the sky.

What is behind these stories? Can the frontier really be crossed? In almost anything we read about earth there is some truth, even if the story is pure imagination. How much truth can there be in stories about space?

Captain Brant swung himself to the outer plating of the space platform and walked toward where two spacemen were welding a patch over the gaping, fused hole made by the meteor. His electromagnetic boots made no sound in the airless void, even though he could feel them pull free from the steel plating at every step.

Brant made a brief inspection. Then, satisfied that the work was going well, he looked outward toward the great curve of earth. He liked being in space, even though his bulky suit made movement awkward. The windows of the space platform, sandblasted by the constant rain of cosmic dust, distorted the view of earth. Out here in the vacuum of space there was no distortion. Earth was beautiful as it passed a thousand miles below.

North America, he saw, was almost covered by bad weather. Sunlight reflected from the great cloud bank and hurt his eyes. He increased the polarization of his helmet glass until he could see more easily. It was probably snowing in Chicago and raining in Dallas, he thought. He wished he could feel rain on his face again. The never-ending sameness of the platform's artificial atmosphere got on his nerves.

Even so, it was better than Mars. Trouble with Mars was that some of the oases looked like places he knew on earth.

You were tempted to walk out without a space suit. But walking into the thin, cold Martian air was as bad as walking into space itself, at least for an earthman. Seeing the Martians walk around without suits made it even harder. The Martians breathed the thin air with no trouble at all, and laughed at the Terrestrials who had to wear oxygen helmets and pressure suits.

That's one kind of space yarn. Another kind goes like this:

Mike Malone took a quick look at the visiport and saw that the Arcturian cruiser was only a few parsecs away. He jerked the communicator switch and yelled, "Rocky! How are those engines?"

The face of the engineer appeared on the screen, forehead wrinkled with worry. "Don't try to use the space warp, Commander. You'll blow us into a flaming mass of space gas. That last Arky shot wrecked every warp matrix in the hyper-bank."

Malone frowned. Unless he could throw the patrol rocket into hyper-drive, the Arcturians would come within close range. He knew the ship would never stand another shot from the mighty alien proton guns. But even complete disintegration would be better than falling into the hands of the Arcturians.

"You'd better rig something to put us in hyper-drive in the next two minutes," Malone said tersely, "or we'll get blasted into cosmic junk by the next Arky shot."

He switched on his patrol contact communicator. "This is the 'Empyrean,' calling 'Sirius.' Where are you, Don?"

The voice of Commander Don Slade of the "Sirius" came through with the fluttering rhythm caused by blasting a signal through space warp. "On my way, Mike. We're about ten parsecs behind you. Can you hold out?"

Malone estimated quickly. Ten parsecs meant over twenty minutes before help could come. "No," he said bluntly. "Don, if this Arky gets us, be sure you get him. We caught him on an intercept course to Pluto. If he takes over our base there, the entire solar system is doomed!"

This last kind of story has a name among those who are seriously interested in space or in good science fiction. The name is "space opera." Unreal cowboy stories about the kind of West that never existed are called "horse operas" for the same reason. Space opera is fun to read, perhaps, if you can get any meaning from unusual words which really don't mean much of anything. But if stories like this ever come true it won't be within the lifetime of anyone living today. You'll see why as you read later chapters.

The first kind of story about the captain on the space platform is different. It could come true within the next twenty years.

It might come true even sooner, depending on how much time and effort we put into problems of getting men to space. Because in the next few years we will learn most of the things we need to know, including how to build rockets powerful enough, and what will happen to men once they pass the last frontier.

Right now, the biggest effort is going into tiny "birds of space" that will act as scouts. These scouts will be fired into space one at a time, starting in the last six months of 1957. Once they have reached their assigned position in space, they will move into the kind of path called an orbit, and they will circle the earth as artificial moons.

The name given to the launching of these first man-made satellites is PROJECT VANGUARD. The name was well chosen, because these tiny space travellers, scarcely larger than basketballs, will be the vanguard of bigger and more complicated ones.

The launchings will take place during what is called "The International Geophysical Year." This is a period, actually longer than a year, when scientists all over the world work together in carefully planned experiments to find out more about the planet on which we live.

Later we will discuss PROJECT VANGUARD in more detail, but it is not the only important thing now going on. There is much more evidence that the day of space travel has almost arrived.

The U. S. Air Force has an active Department of Space Medicine. The department's job is to find out what happens to men out where the atmosphere is thin, and in the realms beyond. It is part of the Air Force School of Aviation Medicine, located at Randolph Field, Texas.

One of America's finest schools, the University of California at Los Angeles, has for the past few years been giving a course in space navigation with Dr. Samuel Herrick, associate professor of astronomy, as instructor.

You may also have read of intensive work on new weapons, called intercontinental ballistic missiles. These great rockets, which may someday replace the heavy bomber, may be designed to go into space, or at least out to the fringes of the atmosphere, on their way to the target. Work on these missiles will also give us much information and experience on the problems of space travel.

One might almost think that many of the stories written about space flight are coming true. Of course much of the fiction about space is so fantastic that the chance of its coming true are very slim, but the kind of stories written by the more careful writers, like Arthur C. Clarke and Robert Heinlein, could come true much sooner than even those careful authors might have guessed.

Stories about space are not new. They date back to the second century when a Greek monk named Lucian of Samosata wrote about a trip to the moon. Since then, space stories have appeared regularly. Some of the authors have names everyone knows, like Rabelais, Francis Bacon, Jonathan Swift, the famous astronomer Johannes Kepler, Jules Verne, Edgar Allan Poe, and H. G. Wells.

Some of these authors made amazing predictions.

In *Gulliver's Travels*, Swift described two tiny moons that circled the planet Mars. He told how often they circled the planet and about how far away they were— and he did it in the year 1726. The moons of Mars, pretty close to the way Swift described them, were not discovered until a hundred and fifty years later by the American astronomer Asaph Hall.

A few authors like Swift, Bacon, and Rabelais used space stories as allegories to give their views on the way nations were governed and people lived. They weren't really interested in space as a frontier. But most authors wrote about space because they saw it as an adventure, or a challenge. Space was something man had to reach.

But space is more than just a frontier. There are practical scientific reasons for reaching it. Because our atmosphere acts as a screen, there are many things of scientific value we cannot know until we get beyond the shield of air.

There is an international organization of men who believe in the future of space flight. It is called the International Astronautical Federation. Members are the people of national rocket or interplanetary societies, and at annual international meetings they exchange information on ideas and progress. The first meeting was held in Paris, in 1950, and there have been annual meetings ever since. America was not officially represented that first year, but by 1951 the American

Rocket Society had joined and there were technical papers given by Americans at the second international meeting in London.

When the American program for the launching of the first satellites was announced, the 1955 meeting of the Federation was in session at Copenhagen, Denmark.

The Russians hurried to make an announcement of their own, and Mr. A. G. Karpenko, secretary of a Russian scientific committee on space flight, said that the Soviets are interested in studying the problems of future communications with space ships. Another Russian scientist, M. K. Tikhonravov, said earlier that a space platform is not only possible but probable, and that Soviet orbital rocket development is equal to, if not ahead of, ours. A Russian magazine has also announced that the Soviet flag will be planted on the moon within fifty years.

So the race may be on to see which nation gets a manned space platform into an orbit around earth first. A smaller race has already begun, to see whether we or the Russians will launch the first unmanned satellite, but at least this race is a peaceful one.

No matter what nation wins the race to hang a man-made moon in the sky, America already has the credit for first crossing the space frontier.

On February 24, 1949, "Project Bumper" took place at White Sands Proving Ground, New Mexico. A small rocket named the "WAC Corporal" was attached to the nose of a big V-2 rocket. The V-2 was a U. S. Army rocket of the kind the Germans fired at London during World War Two.

The V-2 rocketed upward until its fuel was gone; then the little WAC Corporal's jets fired and it left the V-2 behind. The little rocket sped upward to a height of 250 miles, touching the region where the first man-made satellites will travel. Then the rocket started the long, deadly fall back to earth once more.

So the WAC Corporal was the first man-made object to cross the greatest frontier of all.

# 2

# Where
# Space Begins

We are not really creatures of the earth. We are creatures of the air—just as a shellfish is a creature of the water, although it may never leave the ocean bottom. We must have air to live, and it must be air of a certain kind, weight, and thickness.

Air suitable for men to breathe does not exist very far above the earth's surface. Pilots wear oxygen masks starting at two to three miles above the ground. Above seven miles the air is so thin a pilot must have a special cabin which is pressurized. That is, it must be airtight and the air inside must be kept thick—or dense—enough for him to breathe when the air outside is very thin.

The men who have flown the highest are test pilots flying experimental rocket airplanes that are really high altitude laboratories. These rocket planes have gone to altitudes of about 16 miles, and we can expect that later models will go even higher. William Bridgeman was the first of the pilots to reach high altitude.

He went up to 15 miles, but his record was soon broken by Marine Colonel Marion Carl.

High as the rocket planes have climbed, they have not yet approached the boundary of space. Even though most of our air is within 20 miles of earth's surface, the atmosphere continues for more than another hundred miles, far beyond the range of even rocket planes.

To reach space man must go beyond the air—or the atmosphere, to call it by its right name.

The atmosphere does not stop at a sharp, clear line. As we go higher and higher above the earth it gets thinner and thinner. There are fewer atoms and molecules of oxygen, nitrogen, carbon dioxide, water vapor and other elements that go to make up our air. Where the layer of atmosphere called the "ionosphere" ends— at about 120 miles—the particles of air are so scarce that there is a better vacuum than any we can produce on earth, even in a laboratory.

But there are particles of air even beyond 120 miles. The aurora borealis, or northern lights, has been seen two hundred miles up, so we know there are a few molecules up there.

Then where does space begin?

It begins at the point where the atmosphere is so thin it has little effect on anything passing through. It begins above the place where meteors start to glow from air friction. Dr. Joseph Kaplan of the University of California says that the air above the ionosphere is

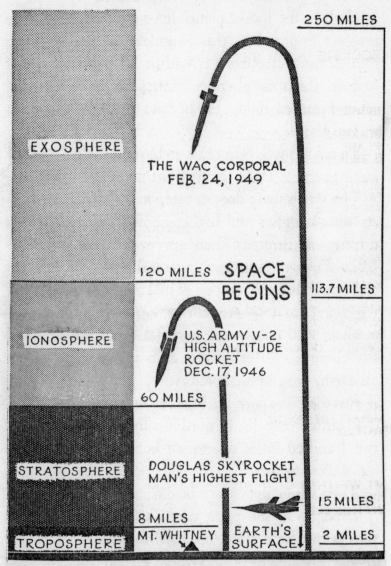

WHERE SPACE BEGINS

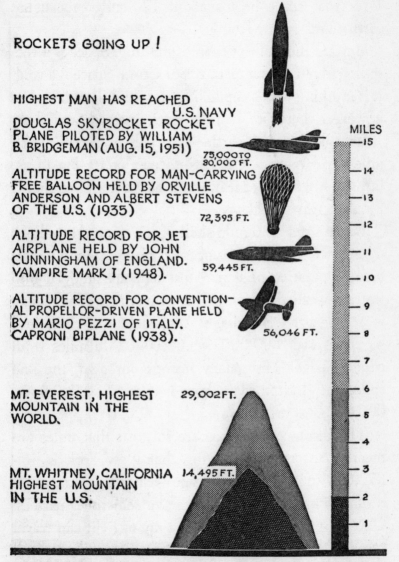

ROCKETS GOING UP !

HIGHEST MAN HAS REACHED
U.S. NAVY
DOUGLAS SKYROCKET ROCKET
PLANE PILOTED BY WILLIAM
B. BRIDGEMAN (AUG. 15, 1951)
75,000 TO 80,000 FT.

ALTITUDE RECORD FOR MAN-CARRYING
FREE BALLOON HELD BY ORVILLE
ANDERSON AND ALBERT STEVENS
OF THE U.S. (1935)
72,395 FT.

ALTITUDE RECORD FOR JET
AIRPLANE HELD BY JOHN
CUNNINGHAM OF ENGLAND.
VAMPIRE MARK I (1948).
59,445 FT.

ALTITUDE RECORD FOR CONVENTION-
AL PROPELLOR-DRIVEN PLANE HELD
BY MARIO PEZZI OF ITALY.
CAPRONI BIPLANE (1938).
56,046 FT.

MT. EVEREST, HIGHEST
MOUNTAIN IN THE
WORLD.
29,002 FT.

MT. WHITNEY, CALIFORNIA
HIGHEST MOUNTAIN
IN THE U.S.
14,495 FT.

MILES
15
14
13
12
11
10
9
8
7
6
5
4
3
2
1

ALTITUDE RECORDS FOR VARIOUS AIRCRAFT

so rarefied that it no longer has any effect. Where the ionosphere ends is as good a place as any, so let's agree that space begins about 120 miles above the earth. This is our frontier.

Beyond the frontier there is nothing. Space is a vacuum without air, temperature or sound. Space is a void. It is Nothing with a capital N. Here and there in space, however, there are worlds, stars, meteors and dust.

Our world—the earth—is a ball or sphere 7926 miles in diameter. The earth seems pretty big to us, but when we look at it in terms of space we see that it is only a tiny speck.

Beyond our 120-mile shell of air there are billions upon uncounted billions of miles of space, with a scattered population of stars. Most stars are grouped into universes called galaxies. Our own Milky Way galaxy is a good-sized one that is shaped like a wheel and measures over 600,000,000,000,000,000 miles from edge to edge. The galaxy nearest our own, the one called the Andromeda galaxy, is over 4,800,000,000,-000,000,000 miles away.

The distances in space are so great that miles are meaningless. It's like saying that New York is 46,-872,640 inches from Chicago. Astronomers measure distances in space by light years or sometimes parsecs. One light-year is the distance a ray of light can travel in one year at a speed of 186,000 miles each second! It figures out to about six million million miles. A parsec is 3.2 light years.

The Hale 200-inch telescope on Mount Palomar can see into space for a billion light years! At that distance there are still galaxies. As far as anyone knows, space just keeps going on forever, thinly populated by galaxies which contain millions of stars each.

Our nearest star neighbor, not counting the sun, is a star called Alpha Centauri. It is about four light years away.

Space is some frontier!

But we should not be concerned with the great reaches of space until we have explored our own back yard—our own solar system.

Our system is tucked into a corner of space near one edge of the great Milky Way galaxy. The most important object in the system is the sun. The sun is a common type of star that fits close to the middle of the star scale both in size and magnitude. A star's magnitude is its brightness.

Around the sun are nine major planets, many thousands of minor planets which we call asteroids, a big family of comets, clouds of cosmic dust and swarms of meteors.

The planets, starting close to the sun, are Mercury, Venus, Earth, Mars, Jupiter, Saturn, Uranus, Neptune and Pluto.

Our earth has another name you should know. It is Terra, which is the Latin word for earth. Note that Terra is spelled with a capital T, while earth is not capitalized. The word appears often in space stories, and the adjective Terrestrial means "of earth." Terrestrial is often used to mean earthman.

Between the various parts of our solar system is the void, which is another way of saying space. Gravity is the cosmic glue which holds the system together.

Gravity is the attraction of one object for another. The sun's gravity holds the planets. The planets' gravities hold their moons. The gravity of a large object will attract smaller objects to it. That's what happens when you fall down. Earth's gravity has attracted you to the ground with a bump. To a much, much lesser degree, your gravity has attracted earth.

When you see the moon you see proof that the earth's gravity—or gravitational field as it is called—extends at least 238,857 miles into space, since that is the moon's mean distance from earth. It is earth's gravity that holds the moon. Of course earth's gravitational field extends beyond the moon. In theory, it goes on forever, growing weaker all the time. But to be practical, earth's gravity is of no account beyond a few hundred thousand miles.

Of course the moon's gravity attracts the earth, too. Earth's gravity attracts the sun. There is mutual attraction between each of the planets and the sun, and mighty Jupiter has such a strong gravitational field that it shifts the sun's center of gravity by almost 10,000 miles.

You might wonder why the sun's gravity doesn't

pull the earth into it, or why earth's gravity doesn't drag the moon down. The answer is that there is another kind of force that acts against gravitational pull. It is centrifugal force.

When a particle of mud flies off the spinning tire of a car, centrifugal force has thrown it off. How fast the particle of mud moves depends mostly on how fast the wheel is spinning.

You can see for yourself how centrifugal force can balance gravitational force. It is necessary to understand how these forces can balance each other, because they are among the most important forces in space travel.

Take a rubber ball which is connected to a long elastic string. Such balls, with elastic strings already attached, often can be found at novelty stores. Hold the end of the elastic string and whirl the ball around your head. If you are skillful you can keep the ball moving in a perfect circle.

The length of rubber is like gravity. It wants to pull the ball back to your hand. But centrifugal force keeps the ball away from your hand. The greater the ball's velocity, the greater the centrifugal force and the more the elastic stretches.

The farther an object is from the body that attracts it, the slower it has to move for its centrifugal force to counteract the pull.

The ball, or a satellite such as the moon, automatically moves to the orbit where gravity and its centrifugal force are equal. We say that a satellite stabilizes itself.

This can be seen by comparing the speeds of the planets as they move in their orbits around the sun. The closest planet, Mercury, travels 30 miles a second. It has to move that fast to balance the sun's gravity. But the farthest planet from the sun, Pluto, travels at only three miles a second because the sun's gravity is so much weaker in Pluto's distant orbit.

Speed alone can overcome the force of gravity, too. An object which travels fast enough can break completely away from earth's gravity. The speed needed to get free is 7.1 miles a second—25,560 miles an hour. This speed is called "escape velocity."

In theory, reaching escape velocity isn't necessary. If a rocket could keep up a speed of just one mile an hour, it could keep going until it left earth behind. But it would take just as much energy, and from an engineering viewpoint it isn't as good a way.

We can reach space with speeds much less than escape velocity, but gravity will pull us back to earth again. To get away from earth completely, we must go about five times as fast as any man-made rocket has ever traveled.

Crossing the frontier to stay won't be easy, but it can be done.

# 3

# The Third Law

When Lucian of Samosata wrote about a trip to the moon, he didn't worry about how to get his story people into space. Lucian was born about one hundred and fifteen years after the birth of Christ and people then believed that the atmosphere of the earth extended on to the stars. So Lucian got his story hero to the moon in a sailing ship which was picked up and carried there by a great storm.

If man is to reach space he must create something that will confine the fury of such a storm into an engine. We already know the kind of engine. The principle of its operation was left to us by a man born in 1642, Sir Isaac Newton.

Newton was one of the greatest men in history. He took a step toward space travel without knowing it, because in his Third Law of Motion we have the only way we know of—at present—to reach space or to travel in space.

It would be hard to understand what controls movement in space without understanding Newton's three laws of motion. Luckily, unlike some other laws of space, we can see them work here on earth.

The First Law of Motion is in two parts. The first part says that an object which is not moving will remain at rest unless some outside force acts upon it. Another way of saying it is that an object at rest wants to stay at rest. A soccer ball stays where it is until kicked.

The second part of the First Law says that an object which is moving at a steady velocity will continue its motion without change unless some force acts upon it. Or a moving body tends to keep moving in the same direction and at the same velocity.

This tendency of things either to remain at rest or to remain in motion is called "inertia." We see examples every day, and the commonest one is starting and stopping an automobile. If you are sitting in an automobile parked at the curb, you are an object at rest and you have a tendency to remain at rest. If the car starts forward, the action seems to jerk you backward.

What actually happens is that you stay motionless a little longer than the car does, because force is applied directly to the car wheels and not directly to you. The direct force on you doesn't come until there is no longer any "give" to the back of the seat. Then you are hauled forward with the automobile.

You ride along at a steady speed until a stop light turns red. The car stops suddenly and you are thrown forward. Actually, you keep moving forward a little longer than the car does, until your muscles exert force to retain your balance. If your muscles don't act quickly enough you may bang your nose.

The Second Law of Motion deals with acceleration. Acceleration means changes in velocity. If you push very hard on a lawn mower it will move faster than if you give it a light push. Also, it will move in the direction of the push. When you throw a ball hard it goes faster than when you toss it. And it goes in the direction in which you throw it.

The "gas pedal" on a car is called the accelerator because when it is pressed down the acceleration of the car is increased. At the end of each second the car is going faster than it was the second before.

The car brake could be called a "decelerator," too, because slowing down is deceleration. Acceleration and deceleration are the same thing. They act the same way and have the same effect on people. The only difference is direction. Acceleration is gaining velocity and deceleration is losing it.

The Third Law of Motion is the principle on which rockets work. When you shoot a rifle the explosion pushes the bullet forward, and pushes the rifle back against your shoulder with the same amount of force.

According to the Third Law, every action has an equal reaction, and the reaction is in the opposite direction from the action.

You've seen motion pictures of artillery firing. The soldier fires the big gun, the shell flies toward the

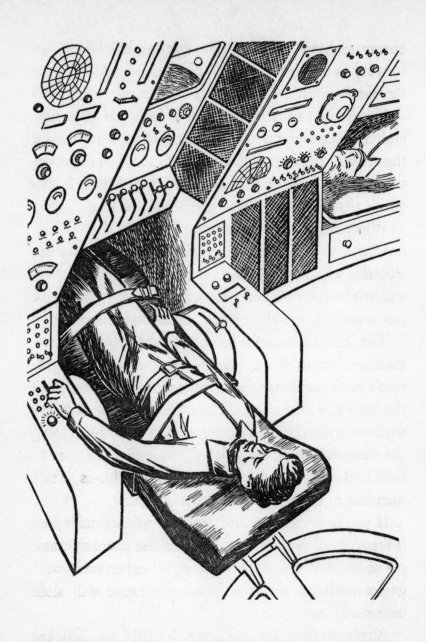

*At the high accelerations needed for space travel, spacemen will be safer and more comfortable on an acceleration couch*

enemy and the big gun slides back. The shell going forward is the action, while the gun sliding back is the reaction. In a gun this reaction is called "recoil."

If you think about it you can see that both the action and the reaction take place in the gun itself. Since the shell is streamlined, the recoil can't be caused by the shell pushing on the air. It must be caused in the gun.

What happens is that the explosion of the powder has force in all directions. The force is so great that something has to give. The thing that gives is the shell, and it gets shoved violently forward. The gun itself can move, too, so it slides backward.

The Third Law says that every action has an equal reaction, but in the opposite direction. So the explosion's push on the shell also means an equal push on the back end of the gun. The gun is heavier than the shell and has a mechanism especially made to take up the energy of the recoil. In the old days cannon used to slide backward with every shot, and the soldiers or seamen had to haul them into position again.

If you have ever tried to jump out of a canoe when it wasn't tied up, you have experienced another example of the Third Law. Dive out of a canoe and you'll go forward into the water, but the canoe will slide backward.

Airplanes work because of the Third Law. The engine turns a propeller and the propeller throws air backward. This backward motion of the air is the action, while the forward movement of the plane is the reaction.

Jet airplanes operate under the Third Law, too. Fans behind the nose scoop of the jet suck in a huge amount of air. The pressure of the air is increased and fuel is sprayed into it. Then the mixture of air and fuel passes flames like those of a gas burner, and the fuel burns at a very high temperature. Burning gases expand. They need much more room than there is in the engine. The hot gases are expelled at a great velocity. Expelling the gases is the action, while motion forward by the jet plane is the reaction.

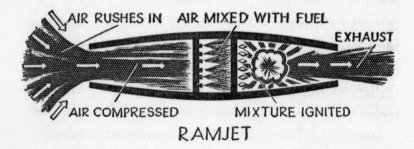

RAMJET

Suppose that the jet engine got its oxygen from a tank instead of from the air. The engine could then run without air and would be a kind of rocket motor. It could operate in a vacuum.

One important thing to remember is this: A jet engine does *not* thrust against the air with its jets. There is no pushing on the air behind the plane. All the push takes place *inside* the jet engine, in the chamber where the fuel is fired and in the nozzles through which the heated gases leave the plane. It's the same as firing the cannon.

A jet engine could operate in space if it carried its own oxygen.

A Fourth of July skyrocket could operate in space, too, if it carried oxygen.

Remember that most home skyrockets are set off from iron pipes stuck into the ground, or from a leaning position against something. Usually they are close to the ground, and earth is more solid than air. If the skyrocket had to thrust against something, it would take off at once from the first big push against the ground. It doesn't—because the jet of flame striking the ground makes no difference. The flame spurts out for a second or two while the skyrocket is building up thrust in its own little cardboard engine. When the thrust of the rocket jet becomes greater than the rocket's weight, the rocket takes off.

Rocket engines have only one opening—at the engine nozzles. The gases produced by the burning fuel push equally against all sides of the combustion chamber where the fuel is burned. The gases push against the top of the chamber, toward the nose of the rocket, with the same force with which they shoot out of the nozzles.

Notice that the bottom of a skyrocket is a cardboard tube. This is its nozzle. The powder charge is a little way inside the tube. The empty part of the tube is where the thrust develops.

Thrust is an important word when speaking of rockets. It means the amount of "action" the rocket jet has which will give "reaction" in the form of moving the rocket forward. The jet velocity, which is the speed at which the burning gases leave the engine, has a lot to do with how much thrust the engine has.

It might be helpful to know what actually happens in a Fourth of July skyrocket. When the power charge starts to burn, the burning produces gases. The gases are pushed down the tube. They are very hot and are mixed with particles of burning powder. You see them come out as a stream of fire. Still, the rocket doesn't move. As the powder continues to burn and the gases continue to rush out, they thrust with increasing force against the front part of the rocket until the thrust is greater than the rocket's weight—and the rocket takes off.

The rocket rises with increasing velocity until the propelling charge burns through into a chamber where colored fireballs and an explosive charge are located. The rocket blows apart and the fireballs shower down.

If the rocket had no fireballs or explosive charge, it would keep on rising even after the driving powder charge had burned out.

The moment when the powder charge burns out is called *brennschluss*. This is a German word. It means "burn out," and it has the special meaning of "when the fuel burns out." The English "burn out" also could mean that the engine itself had burned out, and this could be confusing. The English use "all-burnt" for the same thing.

The skyrocket would keep on rising after "all-burnt" until the pull of earth's gravity slowed it to a stop. Then it would drop again with gathering speed until it struck earth at the same speed with which it left.

There is one other thing that would affect the skyrocket's flight, and that is the resistance of the air.

*If there were no gravity, and no air resistance, the rocket would keep on going at the velocity it had when the last of its fuel was used up.*

By the way, there is a term which can be used for the fireballs and explosive charge in the nose of a skyrocket. It is "pay load." It is this little load which pays you for the expense of getting the rocket into the air.

When an experimental rocket like the big Navy Viking is fired from White Sands Proving Ground in New Mexico, the pay load is scientific instruments which transmit radio or radar signals back to earth to tell the men on the ground what is happening.

When we send the first rocket into outer space, perhaps to the moon, the pay load may be instruments. It may be a charge which we could see through telescopes when it went off on the moon. Or the pay load may be men.

Two words used throughout this book are "rocketry" and "rocketeers." Although neither is in common use, they are handy, simple terms. Rocketry is used to mean all the branches of engineering, electronics and chemistry that go into the design and operation of rockets. Rocketeers are the specialists in all branches of science concerned with rockets.

We have come a long way since rockets first were invented. Rockets were old when Newton was born. Although the date of the first rocket is unknown, we do know an early date when rockets were used in battle. It was in the year 1232, according to an ancient Chinese tale.

*An early Chinese "arrow of flying fire"*

The Mongols had a Chinese city under attack, the story goes, and the Chinese used rocket arrows—or arrows of flying fire—against the attackers. Probably these were simple tubes of powder attached to arrows. When the powder was touched off, the arrow sped away.

The Chinese are said to have invented gunpowder,

so perhaps it is natural that they also should have invented the rocket.

Rockets were introduced in Europe sometime later, and were used in thirteenth- and fourteenth-century warfare. Improvements were made through the years until finally an Indian rajah was able to drive the British off a battlefield with rockets in the year 1780.

This strange defeat came to the attention of Colonel William Congreve of the Royal Artillery. He began experimenting and improved the Indian rajah's rocket design. He also added a bursting charge in the nose of the rockets. Rocketeers became a part of the British Artillery. Later, rockets were carried by British ships. They were first used against the French in 1806.

Then the British rockets were used against Fort McHenry at Baltimore, Maryland, in 1814. Francis Scott Key watched the engagement and wrote:

*And the rockets' red glare, the bombs bursting in air,*
*Gave proof through the night that our flag was still*
*there. . . .*
*And the star-spangled banner in triumph shall wave,*
*O'er the land of the free and the home of the brave.*

During the eighteenth century there were experiments with rocket vehicles of one kind or another, like rocket airplanes, rocket cars and rocket dirigibles. Few of these were ever more than dreams which their inventors had put on paper.

Space travel didn't get serious attention until 1923

when a Rumanian professor, Hermann Oberth, showed with mathematics how a rocket to reach the moon could be made.

There was a big spurt in rocketry and the rocketeers soon reached a barrier. Powder, as a fuel, wouldn't do. Powder doesn't burn evenly, it is apt to explode and it doesn't have enough thrust. Powder burns slowly and can't produce the jet velocity needed to get a rocket moving at really high speeds.

A new fuel was needed—and an American had the answer. His name was Robert H. Goddard. In 1908, while a student, he got interested in rockets and began experimenting. In 1926, when he was a professor at

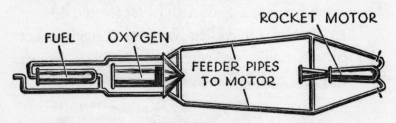

GODDARD'S LIQUID FUEL ROCKET

Clark University, Worcester, Mass., he sent the first liquid-fuel rocket into the air. His fuel was gasoline with liquid oxygen, which rocketeers now call "lox."

Hermann Oberth and Robert Goddard are usually called the fathers of rocketry. Although they never worked together they each wrote mathematical explanations of rockets and space travel which generally are still good today.

A year after Goddard fired the first liquid fuel

rocket, the German Space Travel Society was formed. But then World War II came. The Space Travel Society was disbanded by the Nazis and its technical rocket papers and information were taken.

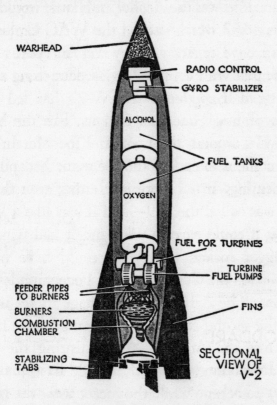

WARHEAD

RADIO CONTROL

GYRO STABILIZER

ALCOHOL

FUEL TANKS

OXYGEN

FUEL FOR TURBINES

TURBINE FUEL PUMPS

FEEDER PIPES TO BURNERS

BURNERS

COMBUSTION CHAMBER

FINS

STABILIZING TABS

SECTIONAL VIEW OF V-2

How well the Nazis used the information is history. German rocketeers produced the first long-range missile, called the "buzz bomb." It was not really a rocket, although it used the rocket principle. It was more like a jet plane operating in spurts. In fact, the power plant is sometimes called a "pulse jet engine."

The Germans called the buzz bomb the V-1. Next

to appear was the V-2, which was a true rocket. The V-2's reached 3,000 miles an hour and went 70 miles up. They were 46 feet long and five feet thick near the fins. They weighed 13 tons at launching, of which about nine tons was the alcohol and liquid oxygen fuel.

It was a V-2 which carried the WAC Corporal up toward space. The Army, Navy and Air Force all have experimented with captured V-2's, launching a number of them. Experience with V-2's has led to the building of new American designs, like the Viking, the WAC Corporal, the Loon and the Marauder.

When the war ended, the Germans had plans for something bigger and more interesting even than the V-2. It was called the A-9—and it was like a V-2 except that it could carry a pilot and it had wings. An even bigger rocket, the A-10, could have bombed America from the German base at Peenemunde on the Baltic Sea. The A-10 was a two stage rocket with an A-9 as the second step. The A-9 would have taken a pilot across the Atlantic. After steering the rocket toward a good target, the pilot would have jumped to safety by parachute while the rocket went the last few miles to the target. It probably will be a step rocket like the A-10 that first carries men to outer space.

# 4

# Spacemen Beware

If you ever have had a dream in which you floated through the air, then you may have come close to knowing what being weightless would be like.

In space you would have no weight at all. You could float in the air just by lifting your feet off the floor, and you would remain there unless some force, like a push, moved you. It may sound like fun—and probably it would be for a while—but it could get to be troublesome, too.

Weightlessness in space has been given many names, all of them correct. Zero-gravity is one, some times shortened to Og or Zero-g. No-weight is another.

It may be a little hard to understand how a spaceman could be weightless while he was within earth's gravitational field, perhaps somewhere between here and the moon. The reason has to do with centrifugal force being able to balance gravity. If gravity were balanced by the centrifugal force of a space ship in an orbit around earth, the two forces would be equal. Gravity and velocity would cancel each other out. There would be no other force acting on the ship or the people in it. So the ship itself and everything in it would be weightless.

It's important to understand that velocity, or speed, has no effect on people. The earth is going through space at 18.5 miles per second, but we don't feel any effect of the speed. When you're in a train going at a steady rate of 60 miles an hour you don't feel the speed.

But if the train sways, or if it slows down or speeds up, you have to balance yourself against the change.

So remember that changes of velocity or changes in direction affect people, but not velocity itself. In a space ship going at a steady rate of 10,000 miles an hour you wouldn't feel the motion at all. And if the ship were outside the heavy pull of earth's field of gravity, or in a free orbit around earth, you would have no weight.

Let's see what a day of no-weight would be like. In the morning you get out of your bunk, very carefully, so that the force of your feet touching the floor won't send you flying to the ceiling. Then you change clothes, and leave your pajamas hanging in mid-air over the bunk. They won't stay there, because the slight draft from the air-conditioning system will move them around.

Washing your face will be fun. If you don't use a washcloth, watch out! The water you splash on your face won't run off again. While you're at it, invent a new way of brushing your teeth, or at least practice squirting water from your mouth so you can hit the drain. Water won't run out of your mouth when you rinse it. For that matter, it won't run down the drain.

After washing up, have breakfast, but don't expect a fried egg. The tiny explosions of bacon grease in the frying pan would send the egg flying. It would be terrible if the captain walked into a nice, soft yolk. Better have boiled eggs, cooked under pressure.

Drink your coffee out of a plastic baby bottle, squeezing the liquid into your mouth. If you try to drink it from a cup, be ready for trouble. The coffee won't run out of the cup. You could shake it out, but then you'd have a globe of hot coffee hanging in the air over the table. If the globe of coffee hit something it would break up into little balls of hot liquid. This is because liquids would always form spheres at zero-gravity.

If you've shaken your coffee out of the cup, you might try drinking the hot sphere with a straw. Ducking for apples in a washtub of water will seem like a baby game after you've chased that ball of coffee around the cabin a few times.

Don't push yourself back from the table after breakfast! You'll keep on going until you hit something, and you could hit hard enough to break a bone.

Feel a cold coming on? Great space! Strap yourself down. A sneeze will turn you into a low-powered human rocket!

Newton's Third Law of Motion will cause you

*Drinking coffee through a straw*

plenty of trouble at zero-gravity. If you wave at a friend the reaction will move you. If you let out a great big sigh it can push you backward. If you turn over in bed a little too recklessly you might spin like a top until you could grab something attached to the wall.

There would be no up or down at zero-gravity. You could walk up a wall, across the ceiling and down the other wall. Fun? Not after a little while. No-weight would be hard until you got used to it.

From the time you are born your muscles are working against gravity. They're used to it. When you pick up a five-pound sack of tomatoes you expect it to weigh five pounds. So do your muscles—and they automatically apply the right amount of force to lift it. The same amount of force at zero-gravity would send the tomatoes straight up hard enough to smear them all over the ceiling.

When you take a step on earth your muscles apply the force necessary to overcome gravity. At no-weight your muscles would apply the same amount of force and send you flying. After a while, of course, your muscles would get used to it and things would be easier.

But on returning to normal gravity you would have trouble walking or lifting things until you got used to gravity again.

It is very hard to imitate zero-gravity here on earth. A few ideas have been developed, but none that really do the trick. So we can't claim to know much about some effects of no-weight. We're pretty sure men can get used to it, and that it won't harm spacemen for a little while. But we don't know whether lack of gravity would be harmful over long periods, like many weeks or months. Some doctors who have studied the problem think zero-gravity won't be harmful. Others aren't sure.

We do know one thing—only men with good eyesight can be spacemen. This is because of what is called "orientation." It means knowing when you are standing upright or "which end is up."

We have three ways of knowing when we're right side up as long as gravity is pulling us. We see where we are in relation to things around us; we have a device inside our ears which tells us when we're off balance, and our skin, muscles and internal organs feel the pull of gravity.

In space, the balancing device in our inner ears wouldn't work, since it depends on gravity or some similar force. Nor would there be any pull of gravity on muscles, skin or inner organs. When a pilot says he is "flying by the seat of his pants" he means that gravity on his skin and muscles tells him whether he is right side up. Space pilots would have to fly by their eyes, because neither the "seat of their pants" nor their regular sense of balance would help them.

We probably could train our eyes to do the work of

orientation. But spacemen might misjudge things until their eyes were operating well.

Dr. Paul Campbell, a colonel in the Air Force Reserve, wrote about a possibility in the book *Space Medicine*. He suggested that spacemen might wear a tight-fitting suit which contained metallic strands. Long, thin strands of metal would not be uncomfortable if made into clothing along with cotton or wool. In fact, some ladies' gowns have metal in them. And don't forget the chain mail which protected knights from enemy swords.

The space ship would have a magnetic floor and magnetic chair seats. The metal in the spacemen's suits would be attracted by the magnetism, and this might give the feeling of gravity. It's hard to say if something like this would be needed. We won't really know until the first spacemen send in orders for iron pants—or tight suits with metal in them.

Sometimes in space stories there are "gravity belts," or space ships are outfitted with "contra-gravity plates" and similar imaginary gadgets. The same idea is behind all of them—that there is some force which can be harnessed, as electricity is harnessed, to overcome gravity, or that there is some way of insulating against gravity as we insulate against electricity.

Such gadgets are beyond the range of our present knowledge. If they're possible, we can't imagine how they would work. But if gravity belts aren't possible right now, there are at least ways to imitate gravity in a space ship. One way that some people have suggested is acceleration, as described in Newton's Second Law of Motion.

If a space ship had exactly the right acceleration, people would be pushed to the rear of the ship with a force equal to earth gravity. And if the rear wall of the cabin were used as the floor, the spacemen could walk around just as they do on earth.

While this idea is fine in theory, it isn't very practical. When space ships accelerate it will be to build up tremendous velocity, like the 7.1 miles a second needed to break free of earth's gravity.

At the greatest acceleration used to reach escape velocity, according to many engineers, the force will be about ten times as great as earth's gravity. This is usually written as "10g."

Ten times gravity means that a 200-pound spaceman would weigh 2000 pounds, or one ton, during the 10g. acceleration. He wouldn't do much walking around. His legs wouldn't carry his weight. Instead, he would be on a special couch called an "acceleration couch." It probably would have hydraulic shock absorbers, like those on automobiles. Or it might have springs that would help to take up some of the force.

There have been questions about how much acceleration a man can stand. The Navy and Air Force needed to know, because a fast plane making a quick turn creates centrifugal force which acts on the pilot.

The effect is the same as acceleration—and it is measured in forces, or "g's," as multiples of gravity are called.

Experiments have shown that a pilot can stand more than enough acceleration to get a rocket into space.

Centrifugal force seems to be the best possibility for a gravity substitute. Centrifugal force can come from rotation. To see how it could substitute for gravity you will need a pail, water and a bathing suit. Partially fill the pail with water, take it firmly by the handle and swing it in a fast circle—up in the air, down to the ground, then up again. If you swing it fast enough, centrifugal force will force the water against the bottom of the pail and you won't spill a drop.

Imagine that the pail is the cabin of a space ship. Your shoulder is at the middle of the ship. If the ship revolved at the right speed, like a tube with a pivot in the center, the centrifugal force at the nose and stern could equal gravity.

This idea has been suggested by many writers—and it would work. But it wouldn't be easy, because of Newton's Third Law of Motion.

To start with, the captain would have to get the ship spinning at just the right speed. This could be done after the ship reached its travel velocity, perhaps on the way to Mars. But when the ship approached Mars the captain would have to stop the spinning.

Suppose the spin were started by steam jets in the nose and tail, like the jets on a pinwheel. To stop the spin, jets opposite the ones first used would have to be turned on.

If the captain used a little less force than needed, the ship would continue to spin, although slowly. If he used a little more than necessary, the spin would slow down, stop, then start in the opposite direction.

Even a slow spin could be dangerous when approaching a planet. To land, the stern jets would have to be pointed exactly at the planet, while a spin would throw them off the target.

In space, where there is no weight, even an ounce too little or too much would keep the ship spinning slowly. The captain would have to be a very good pilot indeed, but a real expert probably could do it.

A real expert could stop the spinning pail of water without spilling a drop. Unless you're an expert, however, wear a bathing suit if you try the pail experiment.

Wearing a bathing suit will expose you to the ultraviolet rays of the sun, too, and you might get a nice tan. But a spaceman in a bathing suit would get badly burned in a matter of seconds—even if he could live in space with no more than a bathing suit.

This is because the atmosphere protects us against the sun's ultraviolet rays. Enough get through to give us a tan or a sunburn. But in space there is no atmosphere to protect spacemen. Luckily, ultraviolet can be stopped easily. Clothing will do it and so will some types of glass. Anything dense can be used. Inside the space ship the spacemen would be safe because the ship's steel shell would stop the ultraviolet.

Streams of electrons, which are very tiny particles charged with negative electricity, also come from the sun. Electrons are parts of atoms. When an atomic bomb goes off, electrons are thrown off by the burst.

Electrons can be stopped easily, too, although they penetrate farther than ultraviolet rays. The shell of the ship would be thick enough to stop them and so would a heavy space suit. So electrons are not a danger.

Two kinds of radiation are dangerous, though. The sun also gives off X rays, while space is full of cosmic rays that come from all directions. No one is sure what causes cosmic rays or where they begin. But we do know that they can harm people.

Both X rays and cosmic rays are hard to stop. To shield spacemen against them completely, the ship would need a very thick outer shell of lead, steel or concrete, which would make the ship so heavy it couldn't get off the ground.

Spacemen would be in danger from these rays. Exposure for a short time wouldn't hurt. But over a period of time a spaceman might get sick. No one knows how long this would take. It could be a few days, a few weeks or a few months. But research rockets that go into space loaded with instruments will bring back the answer long before the first men cross the barrier.

Chances are that mice, fruit flies and monkeys will be the first living things to go into space. These creatures are often used in scientific research.

All three kinds already have made rocket trips. V-2's have carried them 80 miles up. Such experimental creatures will tell us whether man can live safely beyond the atmosphere.

Two other dangers which spacemen will face are meteors and temperatures.

There is a popular idea that space is very cold. Actually, there is no temperature at all in space. To measure temperature we have to measure the amount of heat in something, and in space there is nothing. So there is no temperature.

Once spacemen got there, however, temperatures would be a problem. Inside a space ship temperatures could be kept within bounds. Controlling the temperatures in a space suit might be a lot harder. Where the sun hit the suit the temperature would go up because the suit would get hot from the sun's energy. Where the suit was in shadow, which in space means total darkness, the suit would radiate heat. The spaceman could broil on one side and freeze on the other.

The way to solve this difficulty is to make the proper kind of space suit, which is not as easy as it might seem. The space suit would be insulated and it would have to be air conditioned. Probably good space suits can be made, but it will take a lot of work by experts and it may take a long while.

The scientists of the Air Force Division of Space Medicine and many other experts are working to solve the problems spacemen will face. They will almost surely succeed, but it will take time.

Some problems can be solved now, like giving the inside of the space ship an artificial atmosphere. It may not be as good as the natural atmosphere on earth, but it will do.

If you want to see for yourself still another danger that spacemen must face, go outdoors on any clear night. Sooner or later you will see a shooting star. These are meteors, tiny bits of space junk that are heading for earth when they strike the atmosphere. They are moving very fast, sometimes 40 miles a second, and they become visible about 80 miles up.

Friction with the air causes the meteors to vaporize, and most of them are so tiny that they vaporize completely and never strike the earth. The late Dr. Clyde Fisher once estimated that a hundred thousand million meteors enter the atmosphere every twenty-four hours. Of course most of these are so tiny we would have trouble seeing them without a magnifying glass. Only once in a while does one big enough to survive the hot ride through the air come down to earth. Then it is known as a meteorite.

A space ship, or a space platform, would be struck almost constantly by meteors so tiny they would do no damage, except perhaps to mark up the steel skin or the windows. Only once in a while—perhaps once in many months—would a meteor as big as a pebble come along. Such a meteor would go right through the ship's shell, the way a rifle bullet goes through a board.

The chances of a spaceman being hit by a meteor are pretty small. But if a pea-sized meteor should go into a ship, it would cause quick loss of air. Fast action would have to be taken.

Once in a few years a big meteor the size of a baseball might strike the ship. This would do lots of damage and major repairs would be needed even if no one were hurt. Don't forget that meteors go at high velocity, sometimes faster than 40 miles a second. Even a wad of bubble gum would be deadly at that speed.

Most experts believe that the chances of harm from a striking meteor are so slim that spacemen need not worry. It's something like the danger from lightning. Although your chances of being struck are not very great, if you are struck the results can be very bad.

Next time you're near a natural history museum or a planetarium, go to see a meteorite. And think, while you're looking at it, that here is a true space traveler which has come to earth, a silent messenger from beyond the frontier we want so much to cross.

# 5

# Spaceman
# First Class

There is scarcely anyone today who hasn't seen a spaceman, either on television, in a comic strip or a book illustration. These adventurers seldom look alike when dressed for indoors. But outside, in space, they look pretty much the same, except for details.

Space suits usually look a lot like a diver's outfit, except for the helmet. Some artists prefer divers' helmets, but most seem to like clear globes or cylinders which look a lot like fish bowls.

Some spacemen carry big oxygen tanks on their backs, while some don't bother with visible oxygen tanks at all. Some have little radio antennas sticking out of their suits or helmets; some have nothing of the kind. Some spacemen wear earphones inside the helmets and others have the earphones built right into the helmet wall.

Let's see what a spaceman actually might wear, according to what we know at present.

First, we have to think of conditions inside a space ship. Unless we put the spaceman in one of Dr. Campbell's tight-fitting metallic suits, we can forget about tight pants and high boots. Such clothes would be attractive, but not very comfortable.

Loose, comfortable clothing probably would be the rule on a space ship. A spaceman wouldn't need very much clothing, either, because the inside of the ship probably would be rather warm. Close to the sun, near the orbit of earth, keeping the ship cool might be hard. It would be heated by the sun and the heat of the spacemen's bodies.

Of course if tight magnetic suits proved practical there might be clothing like some which illustrates space yarns. We could call this the "Superman" type of costume.

But let's say that our spaceman is dressed in simple shirt and trousers. The shirt could be the kind that pulls on over the head and hangs outside the trousers. This would do away with the need for buttons and zippers. The trousers would be loose and gathered at the ankles so they would not cause trouble when the spaceman climbed into a space suit.

Shoes or boots would be made of some kind of composition, depending on whether the ship's deck was steel, plastic or something else. The soles would be chosen for their nonskid quality, or they might be magnetized. Simple boots—like slippers with tops— could be practical and good looking.

Let's take an average spaceman who is a first-class

nuclear reactor technician—he helps run the atomic pile which drives the space ship.

When the food bell rings, our spaceman goes into the dining compartment and stands at the table. He doesn't need to sit down. There is no gravity pulling him and he won't get tired of standing. The table is steel and little magnets are set in the bottoms of the bowls from which he eats. That's so his bowl won't float away. He uses a bowl instead of a plate to keep things from getting away from him, too. When food is served it is most definitely not a pill. It is a good meal, well cooked and with about the same things the spaceman would be fed on earth.

There are two reasons for serving earth food. First, people cannot live for very long on tiny pellets, no matter how nourishing they may be. Man needs bulk in his food. Even if pills could give him all he needed, which is very doubtful, he would still need something bulky to eat.

The second reason is that life would be pretty dull on a space ship. This may be hard to believe, but think of traveling on an airplane. For a little while you watch the ground go by, then you hunt for something to read. Bomber pilots on long trips always get bored, unless they are in danger from enemy guns or planes.

In space there wouldn't be the ground to look at and no enemy to worry about. After a while our spaceman would get tired of looking at the sun and the stars.

He would be like a sailor who seldom looks at the sea. So mealtimes would be important. The spaceman would look forward to having a good meal. It is a good way of breaking the routine of a trip—and most people enjoy eating.

After lunch our spaceman has to go outside, perhaps for a minor repair job. He gets into a space suit.

The suit might look like the ones divers wear, but it will be bigger and bulkier. How much it resembles a diver's suit will depend on whether joints can be made airtight and insulated. Probably they can, at great expense. There is a kind of diver's suit, like jointed armor, which is made for work far down in the sea where the pressures are enormous. This kind might be remade for space.

Of course the problems are just the opposite. For work under water, the suit must be able to stand pressure from outside. It must keep the water out. In space, the suit would have to stand pressure from inside. Remember that space is a vacuum. The air inside the suit would act the way air inside an automobile tire does. The suit would have to be made to keep air in.

Both the pressure of the air and the heavy material of the suit could result in arms and legs so stiff that they couldn't be moved. Finding a material which wouldn't be stiff, which would keep air in, and which is heavily insulated, is a good project for engineers and chemists.

The arms of the suit probably won't end in gloves. No material now made could keep air in, insulate hands from heat or cold and still be flexible and thin enough so a man could use his fingers.

Besides, it won't be necessary for a spaceman to use his fingers directly. It would be better for the arms of his suit to end in finger controls for equipment. The atomic energy program has brought the development of really wonderful machinery to take the place of hands. These devices are used where radiation might harm the operator. They are made so the operator can sit behind a thick shield and, by watching in a mirror, work the equipment at a distance. The equipment can do most things hands can do. The men who made this equipment surely could design tools for space. The tools could be made so a spaceman would have built-in wrenches, hammers and other things that might be needed.

The spaceman's suit would have to provide him with air, and the air would have to circulate through the suit. The air bottles would probably be attached outside the suit. A heating unit could warm the gases, if needed. There would be chemicals somewhere in the suit to absorb the carbon dioxide and water vapor from his breath. These couldn't very well be released into space because the tiny jet at the release would move the spaceman. Don't forget he is weightless— and that every action has an equal but opposite reaction.

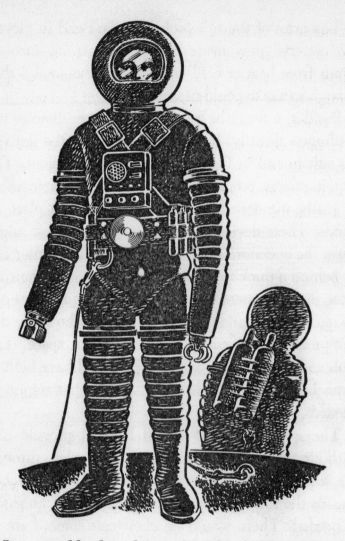

It is possible that chemical packs could supply oxygen as well as absorbing carbon dioxide and water vapor. A chemical pack to supply the spaceman for hours might be carried inside the suit.

The spaceman could walk. The hull of the ship would probably be steel or some other alloy of iron.

Magnetic boots would keep him on the hull and allow him to walk. It would be a good idea for him to have a safety line attached to the ship, though, just in case he hammered too hard and the reaction sent him whirling into space.

A new development in electronics will make the equipment of a space suit much smaller and simpler. This development is the transistor. It can take the place of a vacuum tube and it is very tiny. Unlike a tube such as we have in radios or television sets, the transistor doesn't take much power. A scientist in the laboratory division of the Radio Corporation of America has predicted that a tiny radio made with transistors can be made to run from the heat of a man's body.

The radio antenna on our spaceman's suit would be a little one. He would use such a short wave length for radio communication that the antenna might be only an inch or two long.

A new battery, only half an inch long, was announced early in 1952. It is called an "energy capsule," and its first use is to run an electric wrist watch. One tiny capsule can run a watch for a year. This has possibilities for space suits, too.

If the space ship is run by atomic power, the spaceman may be able to use "atomic batteries" for some operations. Such batteries already exist. They use radio-activity as power. They may be much smaller and more powerful—as well as safer—by the time the first space ship is built.

One piece of equipment our spaceman would need would be a "reaction unit" of some kind to help him move around in space. A jet of some sort which could be turned off and on would be fine. An ordinary "bug bomb," such as we use against mosquitoes in our houses in summer would do very well. It wouldn't move him too rapidly, and he could maneuver as he wanted to. A small flask of compressed air would be better however. The flask could have a grip by which the hand tools could pick it up, and also a simple trigger.

If the jet had any force to speak of the spaceman would need real skill. Wrong use of the compressed air would spin him like a top or push him away from the ship. If he got careless he might go in the wrong direction or bang his helmet on the ship's hull. Part of the spaceman's training would be practice in the use of such reaction units.

It is hard to imagine why a spaceman would need a weapon, unless he had to explore some sky world where dangerous creatures lived. It is even harder to imagine what kind of weapon he might have.

On a planet with gravity and atmosphere about like earth's, any earth weapon would do. In space, any earth weapon would be dangerous. Firing a rifle would propel the spaceman backward with a rush.

In most space yarns the people are equipped with all kinds of weapons. Most popular seems to be a paralyzing ray. There are no such rays known at present, and nothing which scientists have found leads us to believe there may be such rays.

Sound, however, is another matter. There are sounds which we can't hear because their vibrations are too fast. Canaries and dogs can hear sounds so high the human ear can't hear them. So can bats. And there are sounds which only instruments can measure. Such sounds are called "ultrasonic."

An experimenter in Chicago discovered some time ago that such sounds can cause paralysis. An ultrasonic device pointed at a dog paralyzed the animal for a few moments. It didn't hurt him. He just stopped moving.

Sound consists of vibrations in a gas, liquid or solid. There are no sounds in space because there is nothing to carry them. If our spaceman took a shot at an enemy with a sonic paralysis gun in space, nothing would happen. Any other weapon he used would move him backward, whether it be a rifle, pistol or hand rocket. Even throwing a rock would move him.

Another popular weapon in space yarns is a "heat gun." There are many kinds, but they all have the same effect. Terrific heat shoots out in a beam and burns or chars everything it hits. The only thing on earth which produces that kind of heat radiation today is an atomic bomb, and a thin wooden board will give protection from an A-bomb's heat even a few hundred yards from the blast. Some kind of heat ray weapon may be possible in the future, but there is no way of making one at present.

One exception is a "solar mirror," which would be too big for spacemen to carry. Such a device is described in Chapter 8.

"Atomic pistols" sometimes are used in fiction, too, although most authors now know better. "Atomic bullets" to be shot by a rifle or pistol are highly improbable, both now and in any future we can foresee. You may have heard the phrase "chain reaction." It is what makes an atomic bomb go off, and it takes a certain amount of uranium or plutonium. The amount of material can't be small enough to make a bullet. If it's that small, nothing will happen.

Proton guns, sometimes called "needle guns" or "blasters," are often described, too. Protons are tiny particles from the nucleus of the atom. Proton guns exist right now. There is one at the University of California which fires protons with an energy of 350 million electron volts. The "gun" is called a "cyclotron," and it weighs 4000 tons. An enormous amount of electricity is needed to operate it. So this proton gun is hardly an item for a spaceman's holster.

Our spaceman's helmet wouldn't be a clear, plastic goldfish bowl, either. His helmet is made of metal and is closed, except for a small window of dark glass. This is necessary to protect him from ultraviolet rays.

In the future, clear plastics may be developed which can be used. They will have to stop ultraviolet rays, though. Otherwise the wearers will be badly burned in a matter of minutes.

In thinking about how our average spaceman would live while patrolling between Terra and Mars, always keep in mind Newton's Third Law of Motion: Every action has an equal reaction—in the opposite direction.

Suppose, as in some stories, space ships from other worlds should endanger earth. Off goes the Space Patrol to do battle. But with what weapons?

Guided missiles are most often used. These are rockets with exploding heads, guided by radio. A guided missile would take off with a great burst of energy—and it would throw the Space Patrol ship far off course. By the time the ship had fired a few rounds it would be heading somewhere it didn't want to go. Cannon, rifles or bean shooters would also throw the ship off course to varying degrees. The greater the action, the greater the reaction on the ship.

Perhaps the thing to do is to launch fighting rockets the way an aircraft carrier launches planes. But the same problems still exist—and launching the small fighting rockets would kick the Space Patrol off course.

These problems can be solved by proper engineering, so let's suppose the rockets are on their way, and our average spaceman first class is piloting one. He approaches the enemy ship with full jets on—and when he fires a rocket or a shell it only slows him down because its force is not enough to overcome his acceleration.

He nears the enemy ship at high speed. He has to, because the enemy is going so fast. When he gets close enough he fires and pulls up in a zoom, like a Navy dive bomber pulling out of a dive. He'll wish he hadn't. Centrifugal force will push him down in his seat so hard it will crush him. If he is wise he won't make any quick turns.

Even if he does turn at a speed slow enough so that he can take the "g's" of force, it won't be the kind of turn a plane makes. He will have to fire side jets to turn—and a quick turn will be impossible unless he uses nose jets to cut down his forward velocity at the same time. What's more, he can't fire only one side jet—it would just make him spin like a pinwheel. He'll be a busy man, keeping his jets balanced.

The easiest thing would be not to have space battles. But if they should ever happen they will be hit-and-run affairs, with ships taking quick shots at each other as they approach at high velocity, then speeding on past for a few thousand miles before slowing, turning and going back for another shot.

Being a spaceman will call for a rare combination of good physical condition, good education and excellent brains. Spacemen will be "the Chosen," the pick of the young men. They will be scientists, for the most part, because willingness to serve will not be enough. Each man will have to be a specialist or he won't be worth carrying to space.

Many sciences will be needed. Spacemen will be engineers, astrophysicists, nuclear physicists, specialists in celestial mechanics, biologists, astronomers, physiologists, physicians, bioclimatologists, mathematicians and communications specialists. There will be other specialties, too, including space cook.

We can even imagine some new specialties. How about astro-plumber? Keeping the water running at no-weight would require a super plumber. Or perhaps there will be celestial janitors. Trying to sweep up— when nothing will fall to the floor or gather in a neat pile—will take a real specialist. Even making a bed, with no gravity to help the sheets and blankets fall when you spread them, will require new methods.

Space cooks, astro-plumbers and celestial janitors sound amusing, but the problems are real and must be solved.

They will be solved, make no mistake. Man is a tough, resourceful, determined creature. If man wants to get to space, he will get there. If the first rocketload of spacemen fails to return, a second will be sent, then a third. The rockets will keep going until the frontier has been crossed and space conquered.

It won't be easy. The great danger of space stories and some of the articles on reaching space is that they make it look simple. There's nothing simple about it. Before the first space rocket takes off with men aboard there must be years of careful planning. A list of the problems to be solved would fill more than this book—and new ones we don't suspect now will arise.

Meanwhile, much important work is being done. Some of it is not for space travel, but will be useful to spacemen—like the great atlas of the sky now being prepared at Mount Palomar. The wide-angle Schmidt telescope, which is really a magnificent camera, is photographing the heavens systematically. When these photographs are assembled they will form the first complete celestial atlas ever issued of the universe as seen from the Northern Hemisphere. The National Geographic Society expects the atlas to be ready in ten years. Ten years should be soon enough.

# 6

# Escape Velocity

People once said the automobile would never take the place of the good old horse. Besides, they said, man wasn't meant to travel at terrific speeds like 12 miles an hour.

Some of the people who said such things are still alive, because the automobile is a recent invention. What is even more wonderful, some of the people who were children when the automobile was new may see man reach a speed of 26,000 miles an hour and flash outward from earth toward the stars.

It will take a speed of nearly 26,000 miles an hour to leave Terra behind, because that is the velocity needed to overcome gravity. Escape velocity is 7.1 miles a second.

Through the years there have been many ideas about how to break free of gravity. Jules Verne, writing about a trip to the moon, had a "moon train" shot from a giant cannon. This famous idea wouldn't have worked. First of all, the tremendous acceleration as the shell was pushed up the cannon's barrel wouldn't have let the people inside live for more than a second or two.

*Jules Verne's "moon train"*

And what's more, the shell couldn't have risen more than a little way above the ground.

You can see why if you've ever used a tire pump. The first part of the stroke may be easy, but as the piston compresses the air you find your hand slowing down. In the same way, the fast-moving shell would compress the air in the barrel of the cannon until the air slowed the shell down to almost nothing. This is because the shell would move much faster than the air could be pushed out of the barrel.

Another idea once was talked about very seriously. A giant wheel, several miles in diameter, was to be built with its axle tips resting on two mountain tops. The wheel would be spun very rapidly until a car, attached to the rim, could be released and thrown at the moon. A chunk of mud thrown from a spinning auto tire would be the same thing on a smaller scale. The moon wheel was supposed to be about six miles across!

Both cannon and wheels were suggested—but in a different way—in the November, 1931, issue of the *Bulletin of the American Interplanetary Society.* They were mentioned as possibilities for giving a rocket a first big shove toward space before the rocket motors were turned on. This would save both fuel and weight.

Another suggestion in the same bulletin was a sort of interplanetary ski jump. The rocket was to be placed on a huge carriage, like a railroad flatcar, which would roll down a mountainside. The car would be powered like an automobile and would reach perhaps 1000 miles an hour. The track would gradually curve upward, then stop. As the rocket approached the end of the track it would fire its jets and take off, adding its own thrust to the speed of the ski jump ride. A similar idea was used in a motion picture, *When Worlds Collide.*

All these ideas, none of which was very practical, were directed toward one big job—that of getting up enough velocity for a space ship to break away from earth's gravity.

To a rocketeer, gravity is something like a high cliff. The cliff rises almost straight up for hundreds of miles, then it gradually curves inward. The curve at the top keeps getting flatter and flatter until level ground is reached. In the same way, gravity gets less powerful as the distance from earth increases—until it is no longer important to a space ship.

Suppose you could use only velocity to get up the

cliff, as motorcycle riders use speed for hill climbing. You can see that the motorcycle would use enormous power until it reached the place where the cliff curved inward. Then it could reduce power a little. Farther in toward safety the motorcycle would need even less power until—when it reached level ground—it would need very little power to keep moving.

Too little speed would take the motorcycle part way up the cliff, but soon it would slow to a stop and fall back again. That's what happens to rockets. They have enough speed to get a good start up the imaginary gravity cliff, but soon gravity slows them down and they fall back to earth.

If the interplanetary rocket rider can build up his speed to 7.1 miles a second, he can go right up the gravity cliff until he no longer falls back when he stops his engines.

Getting off the moon, or any heavenly body smaller than Terra, would take a lot less speed. Riding up the gravity cliff of the moon would be much easier. In the illustration you will see a tiny cliff inside the big one. That's moon's "gravity cliff" as compared with earth's. The moon has an escape velocity of 1.5 miles a second, or 5400 miles an hour.

If a planet has less mass than earth, it also has less gravity and a lower escape velocity. Planets bigger than earth have higher escape velocities. In speaking of planets, it might be all right to say that the smaller the planet, the less its gravity, but size and mass are

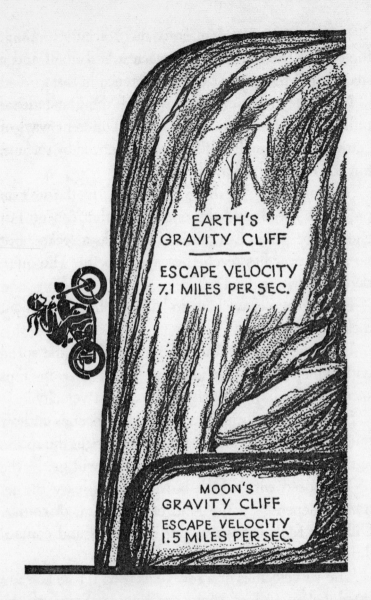

EARTH'S
GRAVITY CLIFF

ESCAPE VELOCITY
7.1 MILES PER SEC.

MOON'S
GRAVITY CLIFF

ESCAPE VELOCITY
1.5 MILES PER SEC.

*The "gravity cliff" actually represents the energy needed to overcome gravity. The amount of energy needed decreases slowly until a point nearly 100,000 miles from earth is reached, then decreases rapidly* different things—and mass is more accurate. Don't forget that the difference between a basketball and a steel ball of the same size is a difference in mass.

No matter what may be invented, the gravitational pull of earth can never be changed. Different ways of getting up the gravity cliff may be produced by science, but the cliff will always be there.

The only way we have of getting up the cliff at present is speed, and the only thing that can go fast enough, or which can move in space, is a rocket. But no rocket ever has reached escape velocity. The question is, can it be done?

For the answer we have to look at a few facts about rockets.

First, the velocity of a rocket depends on the speed with which burning gases leave its jet nozzles. This speed is called "jet velocity" or "exhaust velocity."

Second, the velocity of a rocket also depends on how much fuel it carries and uses up. The longer the rocket jets keep burning, the faster the rocket will go.

The speed with which burning gases leave the jet nozzles depends on the kind of fuel used, of course. Different fuels behave in different ways and contain different amounts of energy.

The jet velocities of a few fuels used for rockets are listed below. All of them are liquids. Some of the names may be new to you, because some of the fuels are new. Hydrazine, for instance, is a chemical made of nitrogen and hydrogen. If you're interested in chemistry, the formula is $N_2H_4$. Methane is often called "marsh gas." If you've ever poked a stick into a swampy bottom and seen bubbles come up, the bubbles probably were filled with methane. Fluorine is a very active element. A weak solution of peroxide can be bought at any drug store and is sometimes used as a disinfectant. The kind used as a fuel is about 85% pure, and is dangerous to handle.

## ROCKET FUEL JET VELOCITIES

| FUEL | JET VELOCITY (*miles per hour*) |
| --- | --- |
| Oxygen and gasoline | 5600 |
| Oxygen and methane | 5850 |
| Oxygen and ammonia | 5850 |
| Oxygen and hydrazine | 6660 |
| Oxygen and hydrogen | 7100 |
| Fluorine and hydrogen | 8650 |
| Hydrogen and peroxide | 2950 |

You can see that even a fuel of fluorine and hydrogen doesn't come close to the 26,000 miles an hour needed for escape. But if we can carry enough fuel we can go faster than our rocket's jet velocity.

Fuel has weight, of course. There is a relationship between the weight of the fuel and the weight of the rocket. If you divide the weight of the rocket—fully loaded with fuel—by the weight of the rocket after all the fuel is gone, you have what is called "mass-ratio."

Mass-ratio is very important to rocket engineers.

They are constantly trying to increase the mass-ratio of rockets because that means greater speed.

The engineering of rockets is quite complicated, and to understand it you have to know mathematics and mechanics pretty well. If you're interested in learning the technical details, your librarian can help you find some good books.

Arthur C. Clarke of the British Interplanetary Society believes that the very best fuels will never have jet velocities much faster than 10,000 miles an hour.

Also, many engineers believe that the very best they can ever do is to get a rocket speeding at twice its jet velocity. That means a top speed of somewhere around 20,000 miles an hour—still short of escape velocity.

There must be an answer. Better fuels will be developed, we can be sure. But the heat from high-velocity fuels is already so great that rockets need cooling systems to keep their engines from melting. Hotter fuels could mean that the cooling system would take up more room and weight than anything else. So better fuels will help, but they won't get the rockets to escape velocity without other improvements in the rockets.

Perhaps we can be hopeful. Science has a way of coming up with big improvements, either in metals or in fuels. Either would help. But such improvements are in the future, and we must stick to the knowledge and materials we already have. So let's accept the figure of 20,000 miles an hour as tops for the present and see if there still isn't a way to reach escape velocity.

The answer is—yes. There is a way. Remember the WAC Corporal?

Here's how it would work. Suppose the motorcycle climbing our gravity cliff was carried part way by automobile. (We'll put a platform on top of the auto for the motorcycle to perch on.)

The automobile starts up the cliff at high speed and goes as far as it can. At the very moment it starts to lose speed, the motorcycle rushes off. The motorcycle is already going at the auto's speed and it would add its own speed. If the car could go 100 miles an hour and the motorcycle equally fast, the motorcycle would reach 200 miles an hour.

And something else . . . notice that the cliff curves inward. It takes less speed the higher you get.

Of course a cliff is a good comparison only up to a point. In breaking free of gravity there is the atmosphere to consider. Air acts as a drag on airplanes, rockets and anything else that flies. But the higher you go, the thinner the air—and the less the drag.

The WAC Corporal rode on the nose of a V-2. Within a minute after firing, the V-2 was about 20 miles up and it was moving with a velocity of almost a mile a second.

At 20 miles the V-2's fuel burned out. And at that second the WAC Corporal fired its jets. It added its own speed to that of the V-2 and climbed away from the big rocket. At 20 miles there was less resistance from the air and gravity was less.

The V-2 kept climbing, of course. It still had lots of velocity. It reached an altitude of 100 miles.

The WAC Corporal had fuel enough for 40 seconds. In that short time it accelerated to almost 1.4 miles a second. Then it coasted into space. At 250

*The WAC Corporal leaving the V-2*

miles it reached its highest point, then started back down.

The V-2 and WAC Corporal formed a "two-step" rocket. It's in step rockets that we have our best chance for reaching space.

Suppose the WAC Corporal had carried a third rocket in its nose. As it reached the velocity of nearly 1.4 miles per second, the third rocket's jets would have fired, then the rocket would have reached greater velocity and much greater altitude.

This would have been a three-step rocket. The knowledge now exists to build a three-step rocket which will reach escape velocity. If anyone wanted to spend enough money and time, it is very likely that the first rocket could be sent to the moon within a few years.

But sending a rocket to the moon isn't enough. We want a rocket that can reach the moon and return to earth again. The landing, the return trip, maneuvering in space and correcting course all take fuel. There are no filling stations beyond gravity. A space ship has to carry enough fuel to make a round trip—and there just doesn't seem much chance of designing and building such a ship for many years to come.

How many years is hard to guess. With science and engineering moving so fast, no prediction is safe. Remember that it was less than fifty years ago that the Wright Brothers made the first powered airplane flight. Now planes that no one even dreamed of at that time span the whole world in a matter of hours.

Of course this is the Atomic age, so atomic energy must have some part to play.

Perhaps it does, but it's hard to see—with what we know now—just how it can help us get into space. It's worth exploring, however, because use of atomic energy is new and much can happen in a few years.

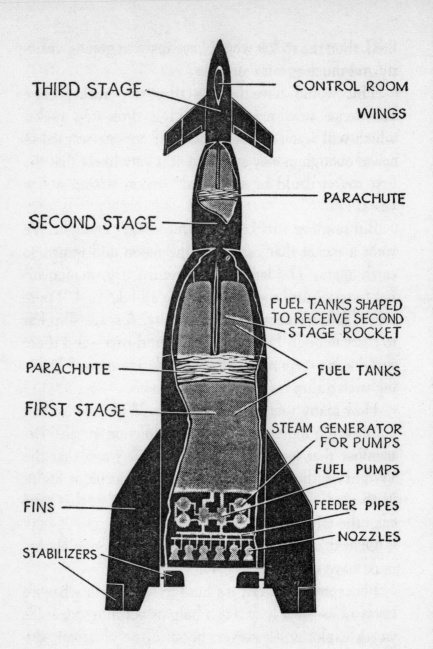

THIRD STAGE

CONTROL ROOM

WINGS

PARACHUTE

SECOND STAGE

FUEL TANKS SHAPED TO RECEIVE SECOND STAGE ROCKET

PARACHUTE

FUEL TANKS

FIRST STAGE

STEAM GENERATOR FOR PUMPS

FUEL PUMPS

FEEDER PIPES

FINS

NOZZLES

STABILIZERS

*A three-stage space rocket*

The key to atomic energy is "chain reaction." This is a reaction where a neutron, which is a tiny, fast-moving particle from the heart of an atom, strikes the nucleus of another atom. If it's a uranium or plutonium atom it may split. The splitting releases other neutrons which smash into still other atoms, and so on.

If the chain reaction happens fast enough there is an explosion like that of the atomic bomb. If it happens slowly the energy is released slowly. This is what takes place in an atomic pile. A better name for an atomic pile is a "nuclear reactor."

Atomic explosions couldn't possibly be used in rocket ships. There is no material on earth that could withstand the blast of an atomic bomb set off inside of it. A big enough mountain might be able to withstand an atomic bomb set off in its center, but the mountain would shake.

What's more, even if a rocket ship could withstand an atomic blast, the blast wouldn't move it much in space. It is particles in the exhaust that give a rocket its thrust. Most of an atomic explosion is pure energy or particles too small to give much thrust—and there is no air for the blast to act on in space.

A nuclear reactor may have possibilities. Although atomic energy couldn't be used directly, its product could. This product is heat. A nuclear reactor gives off enough heat to break some chemicals down into gas. Fast-moving gas is what drives a rocket.

Trouble is, even a small nuclear reactor with all the

heavy concrete or lead shielding needed to protect the crew would weigh several tons. On top of this weight would be added the heavy cooling system the ship would need and many tons of the chemical fuel to be turned to gas by the reactor's heat. One chemical which could be used is water. The heat would break it up into oxygen and hydrogen. Another chemical is ammonia.

Surely someday atomic energy will give power to space ships. We don't know how because we really don't know enough about controlling atomic energy. But we'll learn. It may take many years, but we'll probably do it.

Predictions just aren't safe, but it's more than likely that we won't have atomic space ships until the moon and the near-by planets already have been visited.

Meanwhile the barrier remains. The force that binds us to earth has not been overcome, and the moon is still 221,463 miles away when it is nearest the earth. Give us escape velocity and we'll reach the moon. With less speed we'll stay right where we are, except for one big chance—as you will see.

# 7

# Spacebound

Captain Blake Allen of the Space Patrol turns to the video screen as his great cruiser blasts off, and orders, "Go into force-field drive. We have just one hour to reach Sirius if we're going to rescue our friends from those space pirates!"

We poor twentieth-century Terrestrials are worrying about reaching escape velocity, a mere 7.1 miles a second—and here is the Space Patrol planning to reach Sirius in an hour.

Something's wrong somewhere. Let's see what it is.

Sirius, the Dog Star, is the brightest star in the sky. It's about eight light-years away. You'll remember that a light-year is the distance light can travel in one year at a velocity of 186,000 miles a second. One light year is equal to about six million million miles. So Sirius is about 48 million million miles from earth.

If we reach escape velocity and head for Sirius at 7.1 miles a second it will take us only about 210,000 years to get there.

But Captain Blake Allen is going to make it in an hour. He's going to do it with force-field drive. He might be doing it with space warp or hyper-drive. They all add up to the same thing—special engines that turn distance to nothing.

The fastest moving thing we know of is light. We know of nothing that moves faster. Radio, radar and other electromagnetic waves travel at the same speed, but no faster.

Can it be that *nothing* can travel faster than light? As far as we know now, that is the case. Captain Allen must take at least eight years to reach Sirius, no matter what kind of engines he has, because that's the speed of light and nothing can go faster.

As far as we know now.

That phrase, and others like it, appear throughout this book, and it's important to notice them. Man doesn't know everything. Compared to what is still to be learned, probably he knows very little. This is something to remember whenever you see or hear the word "impossible." Our ancestors thought such things as television, electric light, airplanes and atomic bombs were impossible. That's why it's not very safe to predict.

One prediction that seems almost safe to make is that no startling, completely new way of driving a space ship at speed of light will be found by earthmen within the lifetime of anyone living today.

Man may reach the speed of light on a smaller scale, however. The giant machines called synchro-cyclotrons, bevatrons and linear accelerators are made to accelerate atomic particles at high speeds. Some of these atomic particles have approached the speed of light. Soon particles may be sent through these mighty machines very close to light speed.

It would be wonderful if man could travel that fast. Some strange things would happen. There is an effect called the Lorentz-Fitzgerald Contraction, which says that a moving body contracts in length along its line of motion. This means that a piece of wood an inch thick, an inch wide and a foot long would grow shorter as it gained velocity. It would remain an inch thick and an inch wide, but the foot would become ten inches, then eight, then six, then three as it sped faster and faster. When it reached the speed of light it would have no length at all!

Imagine what would happen to a space ship! To anyone watching, the ship would grow shorter. But to the spacemen inside, nothing would seem to change, because everything would grow shorter at once.

At the same time, everything would grow heavier, because the mass of an object increases as it goes faster.

All this is according to the Einstein theories.

There is one other idea to think over. What is the speed of a gravitational field like the sun's? Does the sun's gravity reach earth instantly? Light from the sun takes eight minutes. If gravity is instantaneous, it may be the force that can help the spacemen get to Sirius in a flash.

But there's no use looking forward to traveling at

the speed of light or faster when we haven't reached escape velocity yet. We'll have to go 26,200 times as fast as escape velocity to reach the speed of light—and right now we'd settle for a mere 7.1 miles a second.

# 8

# The Bright
# Metal Moon

We still haven't reached space in this printed flying carpet about the new frontier, except on a one-way trip. We have been able to reach escape velocity only by using all the fuel our best three-step rocket can carry. If we could stay below escape velocity we could have a bigger pay load and perhaps even fuel in reserve, but that wouldn't get us free of earth's gravity.

Getting beyond gravity, an earlier chapter said, is like going up a steep cliff. It is also a little like climbing Mount Everest, the highest mountain in the world.

The adventurers who conquered Everest didn't do it in one continuous climb. They carried supplies part way up the mountain and made a base camp. Then they carried some supplies from that base a little farther up the mountain and set up another base. Each time a new base was reached, some men stayed behind. Finally two men, Sir Edmund Hillary and Tensing, left the last base and reached the top.

Space adventurers can learn a lesson from these

brave mountain climbers: Don't try to conquer gravity all at once. The time will probably come when space ships will roar off earth into space with one mighty burst of speed. But for now, we can try an easier way and climb the slope of gravity in stages as the climbers went up Everest.

Remember that there are two obstacles to reaching space. The biggest one is gravity, but air is a drag on rockets, too. And remember that gravity grows less the higher we go—and that above 120 miles there isn't enough air to affect anything.

What we need is a sky hook far out from earth where there is no air and less gravity. We could hang our space rockets on a sky hook, refuel them, then continue on to the moon, to Mars or to Venus. And we wouldn't have to reach escape velocity at all!

Such sky hooks are possible. They are called artificial satellites, space platforms, orbital rockets, space stations, satellite vehicles or just plain "orbiters." Call them anything you wish—they are all names for man-made moons sent up to circle the earth.

What a space platform would look like really isn't important. A few that have been suggested are pictured. Each design has points in its favor. A space platform would be a rocket, a ball, a saucer, a wheel or something shaped like a balloon with a string around the middle. Since the platform would circle the earth in the vacuum of space, it would be best to have a design that would resist the pressure of air from inside.

This would mean a ball or a saucer, although careful design could make less suitable shapes usable.

Before we design a space platform, however, let's be sure we can get one into space and keep it there.

It can be done with a three-step rocket. And what's more important, perhaps, it can be done now—if anyone is willing to pay the price. At least it can be started now, although it will take some time to finish building the first rocket.

How much velocity is needed to get an orbital rocket into space depends on where we decide to put it. Orbiters could speed around earth at most any distance, from 200 to 20,000 miles or more above the surface.

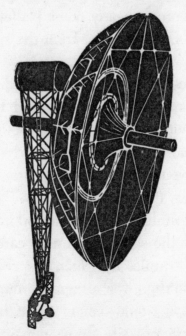

*Ross and Smith's space station, from* Interplanetary Flight

If you think about it, you already know the answer to the question of what would keep it up. Centrifugal force can balance the force of gravity. Remember the rubber ball on the end of an elastic string, and remember that the greater the distance of the ball from your hand, the less velocity it needs to balance the pull of the elastic.

There are words to describe this more accurately: The greater the distance of the satellite from its parent body, the less velocity it needs to overcome the parent body's gravitational field.

All the planets are satellites of the sun, just as the moons are satellites of the planets. Mercury, being closer to the sun than any other planet, must travel fastest. Pluto, being farthest from the sun, can move slowest.

In the same way, the closer the artificial satellite's orbit to the earth, the faster it would have to travel to balance gravity. A space platform 1000 miles above the earth would have to circle at nearly 16,000 miles an hour. It would go completely around the earth about once every two hours.

A satellite could be placed in an orbit which would give it exactly the same rotation as earth by placing it about 22,300 miles up. Such a space platform, if placed over Chicago, for instance, would appear not to move at all. It would remain over Chicago, just as a spot on the rim of a tire always remains in the same position in relation to a spot on the hub of the wheel.

We may have to wait a while for the first space platform that carries men, but the time for launching the first artificial moons already is here. Of course they will not even resemble most of the space station designs you have seen. They will be very simple, probably just metal and plastic balls that contain a few instruments.

*Von Braun's space station, from* Space Medicine

The reason for starting in a small way is because we are not yet able to get more than a small payload into space. But a small payload of instruments can still tell us a very great deal. No one satellite will carry many instruments, but by the time ten or a dozen have been launched, the scientists will have been able to pack in most of the instruments they need.

The instruments will tell us more about cosmic rays, and about the earth's magnetic field. They will give us better information about the atmosphere in which we live, and the effect of earth's shape on such small satellites. They will even help us to make more accurate maps of earth, because scientists can use them as reference points in making measurements.

The satellites probably will not remain in space for very long. Even though they will actually be in space, beyond the atmosphere, scientists expect there will still be a few molecules and atoms of gas in the orbits. Eventually, friction against this very thin gas will slow the satellites down. They will spiral in to the denser part of the atmosphere, and their velocity will be great enough to turn them into flaming meteors. Chances are, they will burn up completely before they reach the surface again. How long this will take is uncertain. The satellites may stay up for days or even weeks.

But all the engineering and design work that goes into the first tiny satellites will eventually make it easier to design and build the first big satellite, one big enough to carry men to space. We may be ready for this big step in another ten or fifteen years, perhaps even sooner. It depends on how badly the scientists and engineers want to reach space.

It wouldn't be easy. Some articles make it seem too easy. Rockets don't always behave exactly as we want them to, for instance. At White Sands, New Mexico, rockets have behaved in some rather odd ways. We might spend ten years building an orbital rocket only

*Carr's space station, from* Interplanetary Flight

to have some little part go bad in flight and send the whole thing diving to earth once more.

Another problem is choosing a stable orbit—an orbit in which the space platform can remain. We have mentioned gravity, but only the gravity of earth. The sun has gravity, too, and so does the moon. In fact, the earth and moon together make up a twin planet system, not really a parent body and a satellite at all. The gravity and motions of the sun, earth and moon would affect a space platform. These motions produce what astronomers call "perturbations" in a satellite. Another cause of perturbations is the earth itself. Our planet is not a perfect sphere. It is flattened at the North and South poles. Unless a satellite's orbit were above and parallel to the equator, the shape of the earth would affect it. This is because the pattern of gravity is not regular. It follows the earth's shape.

Perturbations could be taken care of by choosing the proper orbit and by doing some rather complicated advance planning. Some orbits already have been figured out by experts in celestial mechanics. They are not orbits that follow the equator. They don't have to, because perturbations have been taken into account.

All space station designs call for machinery of one kind or another. Sun engines which use the heat of the sun to turn generators and produce electricity are almost always mentioned. If the space station had lots of electronic equipment, like radio and television, it would need lots of electricity. The generators probably could be made to work, but they would bring a new trouble.

Newton's Third Law again. Every action has an equal but opposite reaction. Any fast-turning thing like a generator produces what is called "torque." In a single-engined airplane, for instance, the plane wants to spin in the direction in which the engine is spinning. Airplanes offset torque by adjusting tabs on their control surfaces. Space platforms couldn't—and the torque of their engines could turn or move them. Torque could be overcome, but it would take careful design.

Having space ships take off from a space platform wouldn't be very practical, either. It would be like diving out of a canoe; you go forward and the canoe goes backward. The reaction of a space ship taking off might kick the space platform right out of its orbit. It would require careful engineering to launch a space ship so that its kick would not affect the platform.

Space ships wouldn't actually have to touch the

platform, of course. They could land near by, have fuel transferred, then blast off without disturbing the space platform.

In spite of the difficulties which must be overcome, space platforms offer our best chance for getting into space. Using them as sky hooks to get free of gravity is only one possibility. Here are some others:

Astronomy from a space platform would be really wonderful. Astronomers on earth must always look at the stars and planets through a 120-mile curtain of air. The atmosphere is constantly in motion and what astronomers see is distorted. Motion of the atmosphere is the reason stars twinkle instead of appearing as clear points of light. The atmosphere is the reason there is still a question about the canals of Mars. We have telescopes powerful enough to answer most of our biggest questions about the red planet if the atmospheres of earth and Mars didn't keep veils in front of us.

Astronomers working with giant telescopes at a space station could learn more about our universe. The telescopes wouldn't need heavy, huge equipment as they do on earth, either, because there is no weight in a satellite orbit and a light metal structure could hold the big mirror lenses.

Adjusting the telescopes would be a nice problem, though. That Third Law again. Starting a flywheel to move the telescope would mean the astronomer would have to use some opposite force to counteract the movement. Otherwise the telescope would keep spinning instead of stopping at the right place. Balancing forces would take a real expert—or some rather complicated machinery.

Looking toward earth through the atmosphere isn't the same as looking out. The atmosphere is like a lace curtain. If you're behind it you can see someone across the street clearly, but they can see you only hazily, if at all.

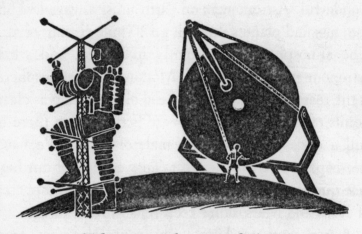

*Telescope on the space platform*

In the same way, spacemen on the platform could see earth very clearly. With good telescopes they could see individual houses in a city. A space platform would certainly improve the maps of the world. If the space platform had the right orbit, one which went alternately north and south of the equator, spacemen could look down on every part of the world at various times, and photographs could be made through the telescopes.

It would be hard for any nation to conceal big

things like ship construction or atomic bomb plants. An iron curtain around a country wouldn't be much use; there would have to be an iron roof, too.

Of course guided missiles, which are unmanned rockets with explosive heads, could be launched from a point near the platform, making the space station an important military base.

From a scientific viewpoint, however, there are different kinds of advantages. The space platform would sail around in a vacuum. Scientists have long wanted a perfect vacuum in which to experiment. At last they would have it.

A space platform would help communications. You may remember that the Army Signal Corps bounced radar signals off the moon some years ago. There was a lot of talk at the time of actually bouncing messages off the moon from one point on earth to another.

Later, the Signal Corps succeeded in making such a message "bounce," proving it would work. The space platform could be a regular bounce point. This is important because there are a number of places on earth where telegraph lines can't reach and radio reception is bad.

Television could be relayed from a space platform, too. All parts of the earth could have a television.

One suggestion that has been made is that weathermen might at last be able to control the weather somewhat. This might be done with a great solar mirror. The mirror itself wouldn't be hard to build. There is no weather in space, no winds or storms. So the mirror could be sheets of thin aluminum foil like the stuff many housewives use in the kitchen. It could be spread over a light frame. The mirror would be designed to concentrate the rays of the sun on the earth's surface.

If properly made, the sun mirror possibly could burn any place the concentrated rays touched. This is not a new idea. Archimedes used sun mirrors as weapons at the battle of Syracuse in the days of ancient Greece.

Weathermen would use the mirror like this: Air moves because of differences in temperature. By heating the air over selected places on earth, air currents could be created that would break up storms, move cloud banks over deserts and make it rain.

The space mirror idea seems like a good one at first. But once the mathematics are worked out it doesn't seem so sound. Many ideas about space are like that.

Perhaps space platforms have been talked and written about in magazine articles more than any other single thing that has to do with space. But in reading articles, keep your mind working. Try to see for yourself why it isn't always as simple as it seems.

The problems of a space platform probably can be solved in time, and the chances are all for earthmen first seeing outer space from the orbital rocket that carries scientists to where the first bright metal moon will be built.

Once the artificial satellite is in place, we will have

the sky hook we need. The orbiter will be the jumping-off place for the moon, Mars, Venus and possibly Mercury and the asteroid belt which lies between Mars and Jupiter. As for Jupiter or Saturn or distant Uranus, Neptune and Pluto—well, don't buy a ticket just yet!

# 9

# Flight
# Between Planets

It takes a velocity of 26,000 miles an hour to break free of gravity if we try it in one tremendous leap. But it takes only about 18,000 miles an hour to put a rocket into an orbit around the earth. The space platform is the key to outer space.

Here's how it would work.

After experiments with unmanned orbital rockets, the first piloted rocket will take off. Probably it will be a three-step rocket, but it could have four or five steps.

The first manned rocket will go into its chosen orbit around earth. Meanwhile, other rockets will be launched—with supplies and tools aboard.

The spacemen in the first rocket will use the rockets that follow to build the space station. When it is completed and enough time has passed so that the scientists have learned much more about space, work will start on the first interplanetary flight.

Probably the first flight will be around the moon, with no landing. Instead, the spacemen will photograph the moon at close range and make other records of scientific value.

A second flight may put spacemen on the moon, but most people may rather have the question about life on Mars settled once and for all. So let's say that the great build-up for a flight to Mars gets under way.

To get to Mars will take little more power than needed for a moon journey. The space station will be speeding around earth at a velocity somewhere between 14,000 and 18,000 miles an hour, depending on its orbit. The Mars space ships will need to add only enough speed to break free. Very little thrust will be needed, compared to the power necessary to reach the space station from earth.

For months rockets will flash up to the space platform carrying supplies and fuel. The biggest single item will be fuel. Thousands of tons of fuel will be used by the supply rockets to get it there.

Reaching Mars will be the simplest part of such a journey. The two hard parts are landing on the planet and getting back to earth again.

Dr. Wernher Von Braun, a leading rocket engineer, has worked out a trip to Mars. He summarized it in a paper presented at the Second International Congress on Astronautics at London in 1951. Dr. Von Braun's Mars project gives us an idea of how great an undertaking the first visit to the red planet will be.

The greatest and most costly part of the Von Braun

project would be getting supplies to the space platform. Huge three-step supply rockets would use over five million tons of fuel and make 950 trips from earth to the space platform. They would deliver 70 men, 36,600 tons of fuel and several hundred tons of supplies and equipment.

*Orbit-to-orbit space ship*

Spacemen on the satellite would use the materials to build 10 space ships. They would not look like the space ships of stories and comic books. Perhaps they would look like a series of globes held together with a frame. Space ships don't need to be streamlined, because there is no air in space. Each globe would carry fuel, supplies or the crew.

Besides the 10 ships, Von Braun's plan includes three "landing craft." These are streamlined ships with huge wings. They would be shipped in pieces in the space ships, or they could be taken to Mars under their own power by adding rocket steps.

The 10 ships would be needed to carry the tons of fuel and supplies. In space, no one-way trips can be planned unless there are volunteers willing to give their lives for the expedition. Each expedition must be fully prepared with fuel for the return trip and all the supplies needed for the entire trip.

When the ships arrived at Mars they would go into an orbit around the planet. That's why Von Braun calls the space ships "orbit-to-orbit vehicles." They would become temporary space stations, perhaps next to Phobos, the inner moon.

The three landing craft would be assembled and about 50 men would go down to the surface of Mars. The air of Mars is very thin and the landing craft would need wings larger than those needed for an earth landing. One craft would carry no fuel for the return trip. It would be loaded with supplies, including some kind of "space tent," and perhaps vehicles like jeeps. This craft would never return to earth. The wings of the other craft would stay behind, too, because they wouldn't be needed for take-off. After about 400 days on Mars, the crews would get into the two remaining boats and rejoin the space ships in the orbit around Mars.

The three space ships that carried the landing craft would be left circling the red planet, while seven orbit-to-orbit craft would make the trip home to the earth space station.

The expedition would use about 600 tons of sup-

*The Von Braun expedition on Deimos, Mars' outer moon*

plies, not counting fuel. The Mars landing party would use about 150 tons.

The whole Von Braun expedition would take 2 years, 239 days. Of this time, 260 days would be spent en route to Mars and another 260 returning to Terra. The landing party would spend about 400 days on the surface of Mars. The rest of the time would be used in circling Mars, either getting ready to land or to return to earth.

You can see that an interplanetary expedition would cost a huge amount and would take years. Think of this when you see a television space hero rush off to Mars for lunch and return to earth for supper.

Von Braun's plan is complicated, of course. It would really be the most colossal undertaking in the history of man, and far harder than the summary shows.

But anyway, space travel is not for those who fear hard work or great danger.

There would be danger, for instance, in every flight to the space station. The greatest danger would come when returning to earth, because of the speed of descent.

Any space ship approaching earth would have to overcome the attraction of gravity, its own velocity and the speed at which the earth turns. Total speed for the space ship could be several miles a second.

One method of landing would be to use the atmosphere as a brake, in a series of what are called "braking ellipses." The space ship would approach earth, go into the atmosphere, be slowed down somewhat, then go out into space again—all in a series of ever-tightening elliptical orbits. After a time or two the ship would remain in the atmosphere and friction with the air would make it hot.

How hot it got would depend on the kind and size of wings on the space ship. In Von Braun's series of articles in *Collier's*, "Space Medicine," and the *Journal of the British Interplanetary Society,* he proposes a winged rocket that would get red hot while descending through the air.

Eventually Von Braun's ship would land at a slow speed on tricycle landing gear like that of present-day air liners. But coming down through the atmosphere would be very dangerous. The pilot would need all his skill and the rocket would have to operate perfectly. If the cooling system failed, for instance, you can imagine what would happen to the passengers.

Another method of landing would be to turn the ship end for end and land on the stern jets. The rocket in the excellent motion picture *Destination Moon* used this method. It would work, but it would use lots of fuel and it would be dangerous. A miscalculation could mean disaster.

Edmund V. Sawyer of the Pacific Rocket Society wrote a paper for the Second International Astronautical Congress in which he said that parachutes and shock-absorber landing gear should be added.

The parachutes would not be of the kind used by

paratroopers. They would be mushroom shaped—or they might be ribbon-type chutes. Or they might be clusters of several chutes.

On reaching the atmosphere the space pilot would turn his ship end for end and decelerate with his jets. Then he would release his parachutes. Just before landing he would fire his jets again in a final short burst, then settle down smoothly on his shock absorbers.

So let's summarize. Instead of happily blasting off in an atom-powered space ship, flashing to Mars in a few hours and landing like a feather, our spacemen would work for months to get ready for an expedition.

Take-off from earth would be in a beautiful streamlined rocket, but the rocket would shed first one step and then another—and only a little portion of it would finally reach the space station. Then, instead of one great ship, a flight of awkward-looking vehicles would blast off—with most of their pay load devoted to fuel. On returning to earth the spacemen would get into a rather small winged rocket and go back to the surface of the planet with a combination of jets, parachutes and shock absorbers.

There wouldn't be many space flights. No private company could foot the bill, nor could many governments. The United Nations might be able to support some exploration, but even the UN, using the resources of many nations, couldn't afford many trips to Mars.

But no one can say what the future will bring. It may bring scientific progress that will make space voyages like those in science fiction possible. It may bring space ships from other planets before we get ready for the first flight into an orbit around earth. But almost surely, it will bring space travel—in some form—within the next few decades.

The term "Astronauts" comes from two Greek words for star and sailors and therefore means "Star Sailors." It is the term for those who are working to reach space.

The Astronauts have been so busy working on space travel that they haven't had time to develop a credo which says what they believe, but it might go something like this:

*I believe that space can be conquered.*

*I believe that I will see it conquered.*

*I believe the conquest will be the most difficult in the history of mankind.*

*I believe that the conquest of space has two groups of enemies—those who laugh at the idea and those who make it appear too easy.*

*I hope and I believe that the conquest of space will be made by spacemen of the Free Nations.*

*I hope that I may be privileged to ride the first manned space rocket beyond the great frontier.*

Almost everyone who works on the first space rocket project will want to take the first great ride to danger and adventure. But only a chosen few will go. There will not be enough room for all.

The captain of the first crew will be a man to be envied. He will be the "Columbus of Space," opening a greater frontier than any captain before him. And, probability says, that first space commander is alive today. He may even read this book and wonder who the first captain will be—without knowing that he will be chosen.

# 10

# The Atoms
# of Life

The great adventure is under way. The first interplanetary expedition is on the way to Mars. Another expedition is preparing. Already the supply ships roar upward to the space station, heaping supplies in the orbit's vacuum for the coming trip to Venus.

The biggest question of all is about to be answered. Is there life on other planets?

Well, what do we mean by life?

A tiny spore floating from a tree fungus is life. So is the tree. There are forms of life so tiny that even the best microscopes can't see them, and also forms of life as big as the great blue whale or the giant redwood trees.

But when we ask about life on other planets we usually mean intelligent life, like the people of earth. We want to know if our Mars expedition will be greeted by thinking creatures who will extend the hand—or maybe tentacle, paw or hoof—of friendship.

To know what we may *not* expect, we must know a little about life on earth.

Everything on earth, whether animal, vegetable or mineral, is made from the same building blocks—the elements. There were just 92 elements before physicists started making new ones in nuclear reactors and other machines. Now there are over a hundred.

The atoms of these elements combine with each other in thousands of ways. Oxygen and hydrogen, for instance, combine to form water. Oxygen and carbon combine to form carbon dioxide. Oxygen and iron combine to form ordinary rust.

The elements are made up of atoms. Combinations of atoms are called "molecules." For instance, two atoms of oxygen join each other to form a molecule of oxygen. Two atoms of hydrogen and one atom of oxygen form one molecule of water.

There are three elements which form many of the molecules which go to make up the cells of living things. They are carbon, oxygen and hydrogen. They combine in countless different ways to form sugars, acids and carbohydrates. One reason they are able to combine into very complex and very large molecules is because carbon has a special ability to join with other elements. Carbon is so important in living things that the very chemistry of life is sometimes called the "carbon cycle."

So, in order to have the kind of life which we have on earth, whether animal or vegetable, the life cycle must be based on the carbon element.

Another important element is oxygen. We breathe

oxygen from the air because it is steadily being used up in our bodies in a "slow-burning" process. A fire that burns wood and the forming of rust on a piece of iron are closely related. They are both different forms of the same thing—elements combining with oxygen. It is from the joining of oxygen and other elements in our bodies that we get our energy.

Plants get energy to live in the same way. Plants use oxygen which they get from the air or from water. When sunlight strikes them something called "photosynthesis" takes place and turns the carbon and oxygen in the plants into starches and sugars. Animals, including man, eat the plants. The animals breathe in more oxygen and the starches and sugars form new combinations, releasing energy at the same time.

Water is necessary, too. The cells of our bodies and the cells of plants must have water. Some living things can go without water for a long time, and some need only a little water. But all living things need it in some form.

Another thing is temperature. The lowest temperature ever recorded by man was 90 degrees below zero, Fahrenheit, according to the *World Almanac*. However, Kenneth Heuer in *Men of Other Planets* mentions a temperature of 108 degrees below zero. Both temperatures were recorded in Siberia.

The hottest temperature recorded was a little more than 136 degrees in Libya, Africa, near Tripoli.

There is certainly a lot of range between 136 above zero and 108 degrees below. But on other worlds temperatures go from over 700 degrees on Mercury to nearly 450 below zero on Pluto.

(Incidentally, unless otherwise noted, all temperatures in this book are according to the Fahrenheit scale, which is the one used on home thermometers in America.)

Earth life cannot live long at temperatures above the boiling point of water, nor can it be active for long below the freezing point of water without some special kind of protection. Some living things can continue to live even though frozen, but they cannot be active.

To sum up, earth's kind of life must have carbon, oxygen, water and the right kind of temperatures.

Also, earth's kind of life—particularly the higher forms of life like man—must have earth's gravity if they are to look the way they do.

We did not become the kind of creature we are by accident. Our size and shape are due to the gravity our muscles must overcome, the kind of food we have to digest and the density and kind of air we breathe.

But suppose our atmosphere had been some other gas, like chlorine? On earth we use chlorine to purify our water, but somewhere in the universe there may be planets with atmospheres of chlorine. Or what if carbon was rare? Could life have developed?

We don't know. Some other elements can form complex molecules, but none that we know of can form compounds as well as carbon. Fluorine and silicon can form many compounds, but carbon is better.

The trouble is, we don't know very much about the beginnings of life here on earth. Nor do we know very much about the chemistry of life in other parts of the universe. It may be different. Everything we can find out through astronomy and astrophysics seems to say that there are no more elements than we have on earth anywhere in the universe, but we can't say how they combine to form living cells.

Every now and then we read articles by scientists who say positively that intelligent life is impossible on other planets of the solar system. Kenneth Heuer in *Men of Other Planets* calls this the "fish" view. To a fish the only way to live is in water. A fish can't imagine life in dry places. On the other hand, a sand flea in the desert couldn't imagine life in a wet place.

When a scientist like Dr. Hubertus Strughold of the Air Force Space Medicine staff says that it is not possible for our kind of life to exist on Mars, we can believe him. Because Dr. Strughold, being a scientist who takes nothing for granted, is careful to say that the things needed for life "in our sense" do not seem to exist. He doesn't say that life unlike that of earth's can't exist.

The people who have written about the possibilities of life on other planets have used facts which astronomers and physicists have gathered. But there is a limit to what we can know about another planet through instruments and calculations alone. There may be things we don't suspect which throw our instruments off and give us wrong information. Or perhaps our instruments are not good enough to tell us the whole story.

For instance, there is little oxygen in the atmosphere of Mars, and no water vapor in the atmosphere of Venus. That is what our instruments say. But do we really know? In the case of Mars the instruments probably are close to the truth. But cloudy Venus is a mystery and we can't be sure.

Even if there is little oxygen on Mars, that doesn't really mean that there can't be intelligent life based on carbon and oxygen. Imagine a kind of man with an enormous chest. There may even be a kind of air storage tank like a balloon somewhere on his body. Then imagine a plant that stores oxygen in a bladder. Plants use carbon dioxide and give off oxygen. There is no reason why a plant on Mars couldn't follow this same earth pattern, but store its oxygen in a bladder instead of letting it go into the air.

The Martian could take oxygen from the plant and store it for himself. Of course he would need to refill his oxygen storage place fairly often. But is this so strange? We need to drink water often, but we haven't developed special tanks in our bodies because we don't need to.

In other words, life on other planets may be possible, although there seems to be little chance that

Martians, Venusians or Mercurians would look like Terrestrials. What's more, their body chemistry might be so different that we wouldn't even recognize them as intelligent living things at first.

Intelligent plants aren't impossible, according to some theories. And if there could be a kind of silicon or fluorine chemistry of life that we know nothing about, intelligent rocks wouldn't be impossible—although they would be unlikely.

We can look at the planets in terms of what we know, and we can say that earth life is possible or impossible. But for other kinds of life, the best thing to say is nothing—and to wait until the first inter-planetary expedition brings back a Martian or returns with empty hands.

# 11

# Island
# in the Sky

The moon hangs in the sky like a natural target for rockets, and you may be sure that astronauts with an eye on the conquest of space also have an eye on the moon.

Not many years ago men thought the moon had an atmosphere like that of earth, and they thought the great level places on the moon were vast oceans. They named them Sea of Serenity, Sea of Vapors, and so on. They even had names for the people of the moon. "Lunarians" was one. It came from the Latin word for moon, *luna*. Our moon is still called Luna, particularly in poetry. The adjective lunar means "of the moon."

Another name for moon people was "Selenites," from the name of the Greek moon goddess, Selene.

Once good telescopes came into use, astronomers saw that the great seas, or *maria*, were not watery at all. They announced to the world that the moon was dead, that nothing could live on it. They painted sad pictures of an airless, lonely world where the temperature ranged from the boiling point of water down to 240° below zero.

This is the picture of the moon that most people carry in their heads today. But is it a true picture?

You'll recall that meteors vaporize when they hit earth's atmosphere. As they vaporize we see them as

*Lunar landscape*

shooting stars. Only air of some kind can cause the friction needed to turn an invisible meteor into a bright shooting star.

Shooting stars have been seen on the moon.

There can't be blizzards without snow and ice or wind, but blizzards have been seen on the moon, too.

Although several observers claim to have seen moon blizzards, there is one who is especially worth mentioning. He was one of the great astronomers of our century and his specialty was the moon. Among other things, he discovered two of the moons of Saturn. His name was Professor W. H. Pickering. He saw not only blizzards, but snowstorms.

There have been lucky observers who have seen faint dawns and sunsets on the moon. There can be no dawn or sunset without air.

So the picture of the moon as an airless world may not be quite correct. We can be sure it has no atmosphere dense enough for man or other animals, but it does have a little air, if we can believe trained astronomers like Pickering.

On the other hand, H. Spencer Jones, the British Astronomer Royal, wrote in *Life on Other Worlds* that although the moon could now retain carbon dioxide and any heavier gases, its escape velocity is too low to hold lighter gases like oxygen and hydrogen. He concluded: "We may expect, therefore, to find that the moon is now totally devoid of any atmosphere."

You can see that the question of air on the moon is far from settled. Some experts say there is no air; others say that there is.

There seems to be little argument, however, about certain mysterious changes on the moon's surface. Many trained observers have seen color changes in the bottoms of some craters. For instance, the crater Grimaldi shows changes from gray to green, with some reddish color each time the sun rises and brings daylight to the area. And there are some very odd changes that go on in the crater Plato.

It's a guess that parts of the moon may have plant

growth of some strange kind, and that some volcanic activities still go on in the depths of the moon.

One interesting thing which has not been explained is the way patches of shadow sometimes move across the moon's surface. Professor Pickering thought that these shadows might be swarms of insects. Kenneth Heuer, in his delightful book *Men of Other Planets*, agrees with Pickering and points out that an observer on the moon watching our western plains a century ago would have seen similar moving patches—herds of buffalo. Buffalo couldn't live on the moon, but strange insects perhaps could.

The first spacemen on the moon will solve these riddles once and for all. We can imagine suit-clad rocketeers bounding with butterfly nets after a swarm of insects. They would bound, too. The moon's gravity is only one sixth of earth's. Although a 180-pound spaceman would weigh only 30 pounds, he would still have his earth muscles. He could make some mighty leaps into the air—if there turned out to be any.

Moon Expedition Number One will have very little trouble finding its way around. Our moon maps are complete, except for the side of the moon which we never see. In fact, we have better maps of some parts of the moon than we have of some parts of the earth.

Of course there's that mysterious other side. . . .

Because of one of the moon's motions, called "libration in longitude," we can see more than half the surface by watching as the moon shifts position. But about two fifths of the moon never has been seen. This has caused many story writers to take off on fanciful flights about what might be found there. Some writers have imagined whole civilizations.

We don't know, but we can guess that the moon's other side looks very much like the part of the moon we can see. There may be some surprises in store when an earth rocket rounds the satellite, but probably none having to do with civilization.

One thing is certain. The moon's landscape will be harsh and forbidding. Where the sun hits there is glaring brightness and heat. Where the sun does not hit there is almost total darkness.

Even though strange plants may grow on the moon, most of the landscape will be jagged, broken rock, perhaps basalt and granite. Sharp peaks will thrust up, while great cracks and fissures will make the ground seem like a mammoth jigsaw puzzle.

In the places where the ancients once thought they saw seas there may be thick dust, like the very finest powder. There will be the same powdery dust in the crater bottoms, too, and even a patch of strange moon plants will be a welcome sight.

Probably not too long after the first space station is orbiting around earth there will be a moon station. Such a station could be useful in all the ways an artificial satellite closer to earth will be, and it would have the added advantage of being on stable ground.

Guided missiles, space ships and supply rockets could take off right from the moon.

Since the danger of meteors would always be present, the moon station would need some protection. A "meteor bumper" has been suggested by several writers. This would be a protective shell against which most meteors would spend their energy harmlessly. They would damage the shell, but would not penetrate. Bigger meteors would go right on through, however.

If a dome were put over the space station, a clear shell could be used as a meteor bumper. Between two layers of the dome might be a transparent liquid which would flow into any meteor holes and harden instantly, preventing loss of air.

The first man-made object to reach the moon, however, most likely would be the kind of rocket called a "moon messenger." Such a rocket would have no pilot —and fuel enough only for a one-way trip. Most such rockets—if we take account of the articles and stories written about them—will have an explosive head so that the landing can be seen from earth.

Such a moon messenger offers a good chance to learn more about our satellite. So let's design one which has a special section right behind the explosive head. In the special section there are six panels.

As our moon messenger approaches the moon, a radar altimeter ticks off the distance. This is a device which measures distance above ground. It is very accurate. When the rocket is a few miles above the surface, the altimeter sends a signal which sets off some rather simple electrical gadgets.

The six panels are blown off. Then, a few seconds later, another relay clicks and half a dozen pieces of apparatus, each with a small jet unit attached, are pushed away from the rocket.

The moon's gravity pulls at them and they fall in long curves which take them some distance away from the place where the rocket will land. Each piece of apparatus has its own altimeter, and as they near the surface of the moon other jets are fired which cushion their landing. Each unit is shock-mounted so that it can land pretty hard without breaking.

Let's examine one unit. Its landing jets blast briefly and slow it down. It hits hard. For a moment it rests in a dust bed, then an inner mechanism goes into action. There is a tiny explosion, which we can't hear because there isn't enough atmosphere to carry it. Legs shoot out and the apparatus is lifted from the ground. The legs automatically adjust to keep it level. Another unheard explosion, then panels drop from the sides. Another, and an antenna shoots into the air.

The machine is ready for action. Its complex innards are made with transistors and other inventions which draw little power. Its automatic control clock is powered by a tiny energy capsule which will last two years.

Instruments measure temperature. Others register

*Lunar rocket base*

water vapor, if there is any to register. Still other instruments test the atmosphere to see if there really is air and what it is made of. Perhaps a television camera, much more compact and efficient than any we have today, swings in an arc across the landscape. The results of all these tests are turned into electrical impulses and hurled back across space to the waiting receivers on earth.

Possible? Absolutely. Most of the necessary equipment is already in existence. There is a weather-reporting machine made for dropping in enemy territory which operates in just about the same way. And the new science of "telemetering," which means reading meters and instruments at a distance by means of electronics, is opening new doors to the future.

Since the moon is our nearest neighbor, and probably the first heavenly body we will reach, we should all know the principal things about it. Here they are.

## REAL FACTS ABOUT THE MOON

The moon goes around the earth in an average of 27 days, 7 hours, 43 minutes. However, because of the combined motions of the moon and earth around the sun, the lunar month is longer. It is about 29 days, 12 hours and 44 minutes from new moon to new moon. Since the moon's rotation is the same as its period of revolution around the earth, we see only one side of our satellite.

For other information on the moon, read THE REAL BOOK ABOUT STARS. For facts on other moons in the solar system, see Chapter 16. Principal lunar facts are listed below.

| | |
|---|---|
| Mean distance from earth | 238,857 miles |
| Greatest distance from earth | 252,710 miles |
| Least distance from earth | 221,463 miles |
| Diameter | 2160 miles |
| Escape velocity | 1.5 miles per second |
| Mass (earth's equals 1) | 0.0123 |
| Gravity (earth's equals 1) | 0.16 |
| Temperature | 220° day—240° night |
| Atmosphere | *Possible, but very tenuous—hardly worth mentioning |
| Water | *Doubtful |
| Life | *Possibly plant, other doubtful |

* Asterisks mean that experts disagree.

# 12

# Mercurians
# and Venusians

"The Interplanetary Council gathered beneath the great Martian dome. There were squat, flinty representatives from Mercury, the thin Martian sunlight glinting redly from their sandpapery skins. It was hard to realize that they were more closely related to asbestos rocks than to men. The Venusians were less alien, however. Only the webbed, twelve-fingered hands and the green, horny head crest showed that they were reptile folk from the swamps of Venus."

Bits like this have been appearing in space yarns for years, the descriptions of men from Mercury and Venus following a sort of pattern. This is natural enough, since science fiction writers usually know something about the planets. The good writers know a great deal and they keep their knowledge up to date.

Mercury and Venus are the inner planets. They are between earth and the sun and we see them only as morning or evening stars. Since they are closer to the sun than we, they naturally have higher temperatures, but they have little in common other than heat.

Mercury is a small planet, with a diameter of only

*Mercury's sun side*

3008 miles—less than half of earth's diameter of 7926 miles. It is only 36 million miles from the sun. Mercury goes around the sun in 88 days and makes one revolution on its axis during the same time. So, like the moon, it shows only one face to its parent.

The sunny side of Mercury is terribly hot. Metals like tin and lead would melt. The ground must be baked, with great cracks everywhere. Quite possibly the landscape of Mercury resembles the moon.

On the dark side of Mercury it is very cold. The temperature goes down to almost 450 degrees below zero, according to Antionadi, a French astronomer who is a leading student of the hot planet.

There doesn't seem to be much chance of life on Mercury with temperatures of 600 degrees above zero and 450 below. But one zone of the planet has possibilities. Mercury has the same motion as the moon, called "libration in longitude." This motion produces what is called a "twilight zone" between the dark and sunny sides of the planet. If there is earthlike life on Mercury it must be in this zone.

It is possible, in theory, for Mercury to have an atmosphere of carbon dioxide and heavier gases. But gas doesn't stay in one place. Any gases that went to the cold side would freeze and any gases that went to the hot side would become so active from the heat that they would fly off into space. So the possibilities of any atmosphere on Mercury seem slim indeed. Yet Antionadi has claimed that some of his observations have shown a slight obscuring of details on the planet's surface. This may mean a very tenuous atmosphere, probably of carbon dioxide, or it may mean that Antionadi saw gases from volcanoes.

Science fiction writers may describe Mercurians, but students of the planets agree that life is impossible.

We have to assume that they are right—if they are describing earth-type life. Some plants might have adapted themselves to life in the twilight zone, but there doesn't seem to be any other real possibility.

Science fiction writers have imagined Mercurians with asbestos tissues, or with a life cycle based on silicon—which could withstand heat. There's not much point in even guessing whether such life forms are possible. It's just an idea some people have had. But wouldn't it be interesting if the idea turned out to be a good one?

# REAL FACTS ABOUT MERCURY

| | |
|---|---|
| Mean distance from the sun | 36 million miles |
| Greatest distance from the earth | 136 million miles |
| Least distance from the earth | 50 million miles |
| Diameter | 3008 miles |
| Escape velocity | 2.4 miles per second |
| Mass (earth's equals 1) | 0.044 |
| Gravity (earth's equals 1) | 0.27 |
| Length of year | 88 earth days |
| Length of day | 88 earth days |
| Number of moons | None |
| Speed in orbit | 30 miles per second |
| Temperature | Over 600° to —450° |
| Atmosphere | Possible but doubtful |
| Water | None |
| Earth-type life | Possibly plants in twilight zone, but doubtful |

Venus, often called earth's sister, is the planet nearest earth. When closest it is only 25 million miles away.

You see Venus as a morning or evening star. At its brightest it throws a shadow. When it is at the right distance from earth you can see it in the daytime, if you know where to look.

It is called earth's sister planet because it is almost the same size, with a diameter of 7575 miles as compared with earth's 7926 miles. It has an atmosphere— quite an extensive one.

Beyond these simple facts we don't know much

about Venus. Its thick atmosphere, always filled with clouds, hides details from us. We don't even know the length of its day.

Not long ago it was the custom to picture Venus as a young planet, probably covered by hot swamps teeming with the kind of life that vanished from earth mil-

*Venusian swamp*

lions of years ago. Artists pictured Venus as the home of reptiles which sported in vast tropical marshes.

Then came the discovery that water vapor could not be found in the atmosphere. The pictures changed. Venus was pictured as a desert planet, its atmosphere filled with the dusts of constant storms. The idea of reptile life and teeming swamps was thrown out the window, and it was concluded with great sadness that there could be no life on Venus—or at least that it was doubtful.

There was good reason for the dry-as-dust theory.

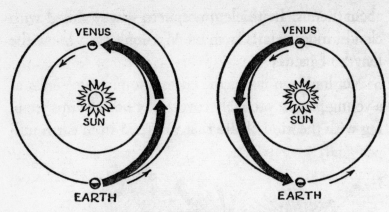

A TRIP TO VENUS AND RETURN

Certain kinds of film, when placed in a telescope, can penetrate atmosphere to some extent. For instance, photographs of Mars taken with infrared and ultraviolet sensitive films show details that are much different from those in photographs taken with ordinary film. But special films used on Venus show nothing. The clouds can't be penetrated. Dust in the atmosphere could be a reason why.

A book called *The Heavens Above,* by a British astronomer J. B. Sidgwick, gives us new hope. He writes about the fact that spectroscopes can discover no oxygen and no water vapor in the Venusian atmosphere, but he is not alarmed. He says this only proves that the two gases, both essential to earth-type human life, do not occur in the upper layers of the atmosphere. He also points out that almost all the water vapor in earth's atmosphere can be found below the seven-mile point —and that earth might look bone dry to a Venusian.

So there may be plenty of water vapor and oxygen on Venus after all. Or there might not be. The fact is that we have theories but very little proof of what lies below the Venusian cloud layers.

If there is water vapor and oxygen on Venus, then our sister planet offers the best chance for earth-type people. The gravity is not much less than ours; the atmosphere is dense, the temperatures not too far from ours.

It is probably hotter on Venus. Not only is the planet closer to the sun, but the clouds would make it hotter by preventing the easy escape of heat. On earth, cloudy summer nights are hotter than clear ones because the heat collected during the day cannot radiate off. But even if the Venusian equator is too hot, the polar regions should be cool enough for earth-type life.

Venus probably will be the third stop on the interplanetary exploration schedule. It should be visited right after Mars is explored. The expedition may find people with webbed feet living in hot swamps; they may find the Venusian equivalent of desert rats—or they may find nothing. We'll just have to wait and see.

## REAL FACTS ABOUT VENUS

| | |
|---|---|
| Mean distance from the sun | 67.2 million miles |
| Greatest distance from earth | 161 million miles |
| Least distance from earth | 25 million miles |
| Diameter | 7575 miles |

| | |
|---|---|
| Escape velocity | 6.5 miles per second |
| Mass (earth's equals 1) | 0.97 |
| Gravity (earth's equals 1) | 0.85 |
| Length of year | 225 earth days |
| Length of day | Unknown |
| Number of moons | None |
| Speed in orbit | 22 miles per second |
| Temperature | 140° (best guess) |
| Atmosphere | Yes |
| Water | Unknown |
| Earth-type life | Unknown |

# 13

# Planet of Mystery

One evening some years ago, people listening to the radio heard a program about an invasion of earth by Martians. The description was so realistic that people got into their cars and hurried out of town. There were mass prayer meetings. Radio stations and newspapers were flooded with calls.

There were many interesting things about the unexpected results of that broadcast, which was Orson Welles's radio version of H. G. Wells's *War of the Worlds*. But one of the most interesting was that a very great number of people didn't stop to question whether there could be intelligent Martians. They took it for granted.

People have been hearing about Martians for years. The big boost to public interest was given by an Italian astronomer Giovanni Schiaparelli. He started all the discussion of the Martian "canals."

In 1877 Mars came close to the earth. The two planets reached the points in their orbits where only about 35 million miles separate them. This "favorable opposition," as it is called, happens rarely.

Before 1877 we knew little more about Mars than we knew about the other planets. We knew its speed, its size, the length of its day and that it had polar ice caps just as earth does. But when Schiaparelli studied Mars through a good telescope, he found something else.

When Schiaparelli found lines on the planet that looked like channels, he called them channels. But the Italian word is *canali*, which is close to our English word, canals. A canal is something made by man. It might be called an artificial channel. Before long, Schiaparelli's real meaning was lost and the whole world knew about the "canals" on Mars. The belief grew that the Italian astronomer had found clear proof of a Martian civilization, probably a greater one than our own.

There are light and dark areas on Mars and the dark areas have been called "seas," even though there is no water in them. Some students believe they are ocean beds which once were filled with water. Schiaparelli found that his *canali* seemed to connect those seas.

Other observers, of course, immediately turned their telescopes on Mars. Some saw nothing at all. Others saw a few canals clearly. In 1893 Schiaparelli announced his belief that the canals really were courses through which water ran. And he said that the regularity of the lines had led people to believe that the canals were the work of intelligent Martians.

As the science of astronomical photography improved, pictures were taken which showed some streaks, although not enough to prove anything.

The riddle of the Martian canals continues today. Some experts believe in them and others do not. Although there is little doubt that Mars has streaks of some sort, no one is able to say exactly what they are.

Even the big telescopes aren't too reliable, because the atmosphere prevents really clear pictures. Both our atmosphere and that of Mars cause effects that distort the pictures. So until we get some new and better way of examining the surface of the Red Planet, the canals will remain a mystery.

But leaving the canals aside, we know a great deal about Mars. We know that it has an atmosphere. Clouds can be seen on Mars. Dust storms can be seen, too. There is oxygen in the atmosphere, although not very much. And there is water on the planet.

The polar caps on Mars can be seen plainly. They are not very thick and as the seasons change, either the northern or southern cap melts and vanishes, according to the time of the Martian year. They are probably snow caps only a few inches thick. If all the water in a polar cap were collected, it probably wouldn't fill Lake Superior. But there is water, and where there is water and oxygen there can be life.

*Martian landscape*

The temperatures on Mars are not too bad, either. By day, in the Martian summer, temperatures may get as high as 80 degrees, although that is about the highest they ever go. A more average temperature would be from 50 to 60 degrees. At night the heat leaks off rapidly because of the thinness of the Martian air, and the temperature may drop to something like 150 below zero, according to some experts.

There are few experts who do not agree that Mars has plant life. Most of them think it is like lichens and worts, plants that are found in barren Arctic and Antarctic places on earth. But when it comes to animal life, disagreement begins. Those who do not think it possible point to the very thin atmosphere—which earth animals certainly couldn't breathe—and to the extremes in temperature.

Those who believe in Martians have two theories. First, there is the age of the planet. It is older than earth. Many theories about the origin of the planets would make Mars older than Terra. Even if both planets were formed at the same time, however, Mars would be older because, being smaller than earth, it would have cooled first and life could have begun millions of years sooner.

Also, the red color of the planet can be accounted for by the combining of oxygen with the minerals of the surface. This is happening on earth. Red clay, red sand, red mountains are all due to the combining of oxygen with minerals. It takes millions of years for this to happen on a large scale, however.

Probably Mars was much like earth millions of years ago. It had a thicker atmosphere and more oxygen in the air. This would have meant a better climate as well as a better atmosphere for earth-type people to breathe.

One group believes that Martians developed then, and that they adjusted to the aging of their planet in the same way the Arctic explorers adjust to cold. The Martians went underground, sealed their cities and continued to live pretty much as they always had, except that they could go out to the surface only with oxygen masks and heated suits.

Another group believes that the Martians changed as their planet changed. Over the centuries they changed physically so they could continue to live even though the air was thinner and water less plentiful.

There is still another theory. Martians could have

developed in the climate they now have. After all, just because earthmen need an earth climate, it doesn't follow that Martians would need an earth climate, too. A Martian climate probably would suit them fine.

Astronomers who have studied Mars through big telescopes will tell you there are no Martian cities. A big city like New York, Chicago or San Francisco could be seen easily.

But who says that big cities are a good thing, anyway? The Martians may be so far advanced that they can have all the advantages we have without grouping together in big cities.

If Martian civilization exists, it must be an older one than ours. Space travel is probably centuries old, and the first stops in space probably were the Martian moons.

Mars has two moons unlike any others in the solar system. First, they are very tiny. Phobos, the inner moon, is only ten miles in diameter. Deimos, the outer moon, is a speck only five miles across. Their small size

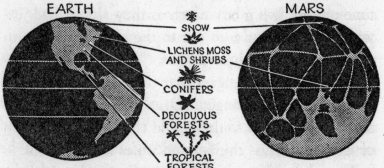

EARTH      MARS

SNOW

LICHENS MOSS AND SHRUBS

CONIFERS

DECIDUOUS FORESTS

TROPICAL FORESTS

PROBABLE VEGETATION ON MARS COMPARED TO EARTH'S

has led astronomers to believe that they may be captured asteroids.

Phobos races across the Martian sky three times each day, taking about four hours each time. It is only 3700 miles above the surface, so it is more like a space station than a moon. Nor does it look like our moon. It is so tiny that a Martian would see it as a little globe about the size of a softball.

Deimos is about 14,500 miles from Mars. This little world has a speed that is close to the speed of the planet's surface, so it takes over two days to rise and set. It is so small, however, that it seems like a star to a Martian. Nights on Mars are dark, because the moons shed very little light.

For stargazing, though, Mars is much better than earth. The thin atmosphere makes the stars brighter. Jupiter and Saturn are magnificent sights and even some of the asteroids can be seen. The brightest stars can be seen both day and night, because the daytime sky is a dark blue.

Earth is a fine sight from Mars. Depending on the time of year, it is a beautiful morning or evening star, with the moon as a tiny attendant.

One morning in January, 1950, Tsuneo Saeki, a Japanese astronomer who has been studying Mars for years, was looking at the red planet through a telescope at the Osaka Observatory. He saw a huge cloud of dust suddenly rise into the Martian air, and he estimated that it went 60 miles up and spread for about 900 miles. He watched it for half an hour before an earth cloud obscured the view. When Mars came into sight again, the planet had turned so that the dust cloud could no longer be seen.

Apparently no other professional observer happened to be watching Mars. But astronomers started making guesses about what Saeki saw. Dust storms, they said, or clouds of ice crystals.

Astronomer Saeki said it was no ordinary Martian cloud. He thought it must be from a terrific explosion.

No one knows what caused the cloud. But we might let our imaginations soar to where a Martian astronomer is looking through a telescope at the lovely evening star, earth. Perhaps he sees a sudden eruption of dust, too. Then, if he is watching a week later, he might see another in the same place.

The Martian wonders what might cause the clouds. They are not ordinary earth clouds. He has seen lots of those. It is not the cloud from a volcano. He scratches his head—if he has fingers or our kind of head—and wonders and wonders.

The Martian astronomer doesn't know he is looking at the state of Nevada, and he doesn't know that during the spring or fall a whole series of atomic blasts may be set off. The atomic proving ground is a very dusty place and the dust cloud spreads for miles.

Of course this is not to say that the Martians are exploding atomic bombs. We don't know what caused the Martian cloud. But we can imagine a Martian expert saying, "It must be a series of storms peculiar to that area. After all, there *can't* be life on earth. The atmosphere is too dense—and besides, the planet is much too warm for our kind of life."

## REAL FACTS ABOUT MARS

| | |
|---|---|
| Mean distance from the sun | 141.5 million miles |
| Greatest distance from earth | 248 million miles |
| Least distance from earth | 35 million miles |
| Diameter | 4220 miles |
| Escape velocity | 3.2 miles per second |
| Mass (earth's equals 1) | 0.108 |
| Gravity (earth's equals 1) | 0.38 |
| Length of year | 687 earth-days |
| Length of day | 24.6 hours |
| Number of moons | 2 |
| Speed in orbit | 15 miles per second |
| Temperature | 60° day, —150° night |
| Atmosphere | Yes |
| Water | Yes |
| Earth-type life | Plants, yes; animals, probably not. |

# 14

## Space Junk

We speak of empty space and we say that it is just Nothing, with occasional stars and worlds in odd corners. But here and there between the stars and the worlds there is space junk, cosmic debris which may cause trouble or high adventure for spacemen.

First, there are the comets. They look pretty solid when we see them near the sun, and articles have been written on how disastrous it would be if a comet struck earth. But a comet is mostly what might be called space fuzz. It has a core of what astronomers think might be rocks, frozen gases, and other oddments. Surrounding the core, or nucleus, are envelopes of very tenuous gas.

As the comet nears the sun, radiation pressure pushes against the comet's head and a tail forms. Sometimes these comet tails are millions of miles long. Sometimes there is more than one tail. But the tails are only particles of gas with lots of space between. Earth has passed through comet tails at least twice. One time, no one noticed anything unusual. Another time, observers thought the sky glowed a little more than usual.

Trailing comets and trying to find out where they

came from and how they were formed will be a good project for spacemen when space travel reaches high enough speeds. We already have the orbits of some comets plotted. Once we get into space we can locate some of our old friends fairly easily. But there are some comets with such long orbits that we have seen them only once in recorded history. Tracking them down will keep the Space Patrol pretty busy.

We need not consider comets except as objects of interest. If they carry any life, it must be in the form of very hardy spores which can stand the bitter cold. But even this is very improbable. We'll know more about the possibilities when we find out how comets were formed.

Meteors are a different story. Sometimes comets have broken up, and in their orbits there are now meteor swarms. A number of meteor swarms move in definite paths, returning to earth at about the same time every year. (For a list of meteor showers and their dates, see the REAL BOOK ABOUT STARS.)

We can picture a meteor swarm as thousands upon thousands of tiny particles of stone or iron sailing through space in a mass. The smallest are like motes of dust. Some may be pea size, and some as big as golf balls, although these would be rare. It would mean trouble for a space ship to run through a meteor swarm. At the very least, the hull would get a good sandblasting, and at worst some of the big meteors would drive right through the ship. It would depend on whether the ship moved with or against the swarm.

Fortunately, most meteor swarms do not seem to move in the same plane as the planets. Once the biggest swarms are well charted, it should be easy to avoid them. The danger will be from swarms that we don't know about. We can identify only those which cross earth's orbit and show up as meteor showers when they strike our atmosphere.

Also called space junk by some writers, but in an entirely different class from comets and meteors, are the asteroids. The name means "little star," but it is not very accurate. Asteroids are not stars, but little

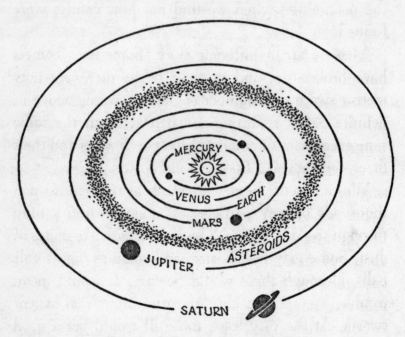

*The asteroid (or planetoid) belt*

planets. They go around the sun just as the major planets do.

If you have seen a chart of the solar system you may have noticed the big gap between Mars and Jupiter. This is the planetoid belt, to call the little worlds by their right name. The first one was discovered, by accident, in 1801. The Italian astronomer Piazzi, who was making a catalogue of the skies, found it on New Year's night. He named it Ceres. It was a tiny world with a diameter of only 480 miles. During the next few years Pallas, Juno and Vesta were discovered and named. They are still the biggest of the planetoids.

Since then, many planetoids have been discovered every year. We now know of more than 1500 with definite orbits, while about 5000 more have been seen but not charted. No one knows how many of these minor planets there are. One authority (Leuschner) believes there may be over 50,000 of them. They range from Ceres down to little worlds possibly no bigger than our largest aircraft. Some may be even smaller.

Science fiction writers have had a fine time exploring the asteroid belt. Perhaps most popular is the story about prospecting among the minor planets. The spacemen try to find planetoids which contain valuable minerals.

Some asteroid belt stories deal with strange forms of life. Certainly earth life isn't possible on an asteroid

*Driving an asteroid to earth*

which has no air and little gravity. But weird plants that have adapted themselves to absolute zero temperatures and little sunlight *might* be able to grow. It isn't possible according to the knowledge we have, but in talking about space we must remember that we certainly don't know everything, particularly about how life may have developed on other worlds.

While we're waiting for an exploration party to find out about planetoid plants we can enjoy science fiction yarns about the asteroid belt. This rocky part of the solar system makes a good setting for stories because we know so little about it and can imagine so much.

## REAL FACTS ABOUT THE "BIG FOUR" ASTEROIDS

CERES: Largest of the minor planets, diameter 480 miles, discovered by Giuseppe Piazzi of Italy, 1801.

PALLAS: Second planetoid to be discovered, diameter 305 miles, discovered by Dr. Heinrich Olbers of Germany, 1802.

JUNO: Third planetoid to be discovered, diameter 120 miles, discovered by Harding, 1804.

VESTA: Last of the "Big Four," diameter 240 miles, also discovered by Olbers, in 1807. Vesta is the only asteroid which can be seen with the naked eye if an observer has very good eyesight, perfect weather and knows just where to look. It is the brightest—although not the largest—of the "Big Four." It is a light orange color.

# 15

# The Frozen Giants

Two of the finest sights in the sky as seen through a small telescope are the two greatest planets, Jupiter and Saturn. Bright Jupiter has four large moons which can be seen through good binoculars. It has eight other moons that can't be seen so easily. And Saturn has its rings, which makes it the only object of its kind in the solar system.

In space stories spacemen are forever blasting off to Jupiter or Saturn or their largest moons. The big moons are so important that they are the subject of a separate chapter. This one is about the planets themselves.

These planets have a lot in common. Both are much bigger than the other worlds of the solar system. Jupiter has a diameter of 88,698 miles, Saturn 75,000 miles. Compare these figures with earth's 7926 miles.

However, much of the apparent diameters of these great planets is gas. They have very extensive atmospheres, made up mostly of ammonia and methane, neither of which will support life.

Jupiter has an atmosphere thousands of miles thick, while Saturn's is even thicker. Beneath the atmospheres, many experts think, is mushy ice. It is not water ice, but frozen gases, pressed into almost solid form by the sheer weight of thousands of miles of ammonia and methane. No one can say how deep the ice mush is, but it makes the landing of a space ship impossible. Also, the pressure of the atmosphere probably would crush any space ship which tried to make a landing.

By using our imaginations to create life forms that we cannot have here on earth, we can believe that Mars, Venus and even Mercury may have life of some kind. But it is almost impossible to imagine anything that could live on the giant planets.

Living things can survive cold much better than heat, and it is not unusual for creatures like fish to be frozen solid without dying. But as the temperature goes down, activity gets less and less until all processes slow almost to a stop, or in some cases actually stop. We can imagine life forms that live in temperatures like that of boiling water, but it is hard to imagine anything lively existing in an ice cube.

So we can accept, until better evidence is forthcoming, the theory that Jupiter and Saturn are frozen worlds where nothing lives and where no earth space ship will land unless caught in the terrific gravitational fields. This would mean disaster. Escape velocity for Jupiter is 38 miles a second, and for Saturn

23 miles a second. Contrast these with earth's 7.1 miles a second, which hasn't yet been reached. We would have to go almost six times as fast as earth's escape velocity to get free from Jupiter—and we simply couldn't do it. At least we couldn't do it within any future we can foresee.

These facts hold for Uranus and Neptune, the two giants beyond Saturn's orbit. Uranus has an escape velocity of 14 miles per second and Neptune 15 miles per second. Both have atmospheres like Jupiter and Saturn which cannot support earth life.

You can see that we're limited to Mercury, Venus and Mars for landing places, with the possible exception of Pluto. This dark planet is so far from the sun that it gets almost no light or heat. The sun looks like a very bright star, so far away that no disk can be seen.

We know little about Pluto, but by all the laws of physics it is the coldest planet of all. The temperature must be close to absolute zero—which is as cold as anything can get. If Pluto has an atmosphere, it is lying on the planet in fields of ice and snow.

Even the size of Pluto is uncertain. Calculations show that it may have about the same mass as the earth or Venus, but that doesn't mean it is the same size. It may have a moon, but we haven't been able to see it.

Pluto often appears in science fiction stories as the

last outpost of the solar system. It probably is, although a planet beyond Pluto is possible in theory. The writers who use Pluto as an outpost usually accept the planet as it is, cold beyond description, dark and dreary.

Among the planets beyond the asteroid belt, Saturn offers the best hope for unusual adventure. It is the same kind of adventure to be found in the asteroid belt, except on a smaller scale—prospecting in Saturn's rings.

Experts have different opinions on the rings. Most of them agree that they are made up of many particles. Sometimes the pieces that compose the rings are called "moonlets," because each follows an orbit around the planet like a tiny moon.

However, Dr. Gerard Kuiper, one of the most distinguished astronomers of our time, points to the rings as an example of a nebula that didn't condense into a planet or a moon. A nebula is a great mass of gas. So if we accept Dr. Kuiper's theory, exploration in the rings is just a figment of a writer's imagination.

Another theory is that the rings were formed from a moon that broke up into millions of pieces.

From the point of view of exploring space, we can hope that the latter theory is the right one. That gives us a chance for prospecting among the rings. But no matter which theory turns out to be correct, Saturn will remain the most unusual object in the sky.

# REAL FACTS ABOUT THE OUTER PLANETS

|  | Jupiter | Saturn | Uranus | Neptune | Pluto |
|---|---|---|---|---|---|
| Mean dist. fr. sun, millions of miles | 483.3 | 886 | 1783 | 2793 | 3675 |
| Greatest dist. fr. earth millions of miles | 600 | 1028 | 1960 | 2910 | 3600 |
| Least dist. fr. earth, millions of miles | 367 | 744 | 1606 | 2677 | 3200 |
| Diameter, thousands of miles | 89,000 | 75,000 | 31,000 | 28,000 | 6,300 |
| Escape velocity, miles per second | 38 | 23 | 14 | 15 | ? |
| Mass (earth's 1) | 317.1 | 94.9 | 14.65 | 17.16 | 0.83? |
| Gravity (earth's 1) | 2.64 | 1.17 | 0.92 | 1.12 | ? |
| Length of year in earth years | 11.86 | 29.46 | 84 | 164.8 | 248.4 |
| Length of day in hours | 9.9 | 10.2 | 10.7 | 15.8 | ? |
| Number of moons | 12 | 9 | 5 | 2 | ? |
| Speed in orbit miles per second | 8.1 | 6.0 | 4.2 | 3.4 | 3.0 |
| Temperature | —216° | —243° | —300° | —330° | —348° |

| Atmosphere | Yes | Yes | Yes | Yes | No |
| Water | No | No | No | No | No |
| Earth-type life | No | No | No | No | No |

# 16

# Thirty-two Worlds
# to Explore

We of earth admire our moon. It probably frightened cave men somewhat, but as ages passed it became an object of wonder and admiration rather than fear. Poets wrote verse about it. Song writers wrote songs about it.

We can be proud of our moon. It's the biggest in relation to the size of its planet. But to a being from the outer planets, this would seem like common home-town pride. We can imagine a Saturnian or a Jovian saying scornfully, "What, only one moon?"

Earth is the only planet with a single moon. The rest either have no moon at all or they have more than one. All together, the nine planets of the solar system have 32 moons. They range from little mountains, like Deimos of Mars, to great Titan of Saturn, which is larger than Mercury.

Mercury and Venus are moonless and we're not sure about Pluto. Earth has one fine satellite. Mars has two little ones. Neptune has a big one and a small one.

Uranus has five, ranging from small to medium. Saturn has ten, including the biggest moon of all, and great Jupiter has an even dozen.

These moons are important to space travel because each is a possible space station for use when interplanetary exploration begins. Some of the moons are pretty big worlds in their own right and no study of the solar system would be complete without them.

Moons have advantages as space stations. They are stable, so that a space ship blast won't disturb them as it might a space platform. Some of them probably have minerals that would be useful in constructing a station, or even in repairing or refueling ships. Since they have low gravity, it doesn't take much precious fuel to blast off from one.

These advantages are true of even the small moons —and some of them are pretty tiny. In fact, moons can be divided into two groups, those little ones that are probably captured asteroids and those which were formed when their planets were.

Deimos and Phobos, for instance, probably were once planetoids. Their orbits took them too close to Mars and the red planet's gravity captured them. At least that is the theory, and it sounds reasonable because the two moons are so small.

Some of Jupiter's dozen moons were probably asteroids, too. Practically everything in the solar system moves counterclockwise, as seen from the celestial north pole. Jupiter's three outer moons are exceptions. They are called "retrograde moons."

Perhaps the fact that Jupiter does have moons which go "backward" is evidence that they once were asteroids. A planet with Jupiter's powerful gravitational field could capture an unwary asteroid easily, and the minor planet could be thrown into an orbit going in either direction.

*Space ship orbiting Saturn*

There is only one difficulty in pointing to Jupiter's retrograde moons as evidence of captured asteroids— Neptune's big moon, Triton, is also retrograde, and it's far too great ever to have been a minor planet.

It's possible that Jupiter has more moons than we've discovered. In fact, some astronomers think it very likely that Jupiter has a family of captured asteroids, all smaller than Deimos or Phobos and all too small to be picked up in our telescopes.

Saturn could have captured asteroids, too, because some minor planet orbits go out past Saturn. But there is no particular evidence that any of the ringed planet's moons are captives.

However, Neptune, which couldn't have captured an asteroid because it's too far beyond the belt, may have captured something even more unusual. We don't know what it is. Its name is Nereid, and it was discovered in 1949 by Dr. Gerard Kuiper. Nereid has an orbit unlike that of any other moon. It is a very elongated ellipse that takes it a million miles from Neptune on one end and five million miles on the other. Willy Ley, probably the best known writer on rockets and rocket ships, points out in an article in *Galaxy* Magazine that this kind of orbit is "of a type considered *characteristic of comets.*"

If we agree that almost any moon could be used as a space station, we have a large choice. Either Deimos or Phobos would be useful, but it would depend on what was wanted. For refueling and general use as a way station to or from the surface of Mars, Phobos probably would be best. Its rapid rate of travel wouldn't interfere with operations and it is very close to the surface of the planet.

Although Deimos is farther away, it travels at a better speed for observation. If spacemen just wanted a station from which to take a long look at Mars, an observatory on Deimos would give them many hours of looking at just one place on the planet's surface.

The moons of Jupiter offer an even wider choice and some exciting possibilities. The Jovian moons—the adjective means "of Jove," which is another name for Jupiter in mythology—have numbers. The numbers show their order of discovery.

*Jupiter and its four largest moons*

Galileo discovered the first four in 1610 and they were named Io, Europa, Ganymede and Callisto, Nos. I, II, III and IV. Nameless No. V is closest to the planet with a mean distance of 112,600 miles. Although only half as far from Jupiter as our moon is to earth, V wouldn't look like very much to a Jovian. It is only 100 miles in diameter, so that it would seem like a large star.

These are Jupiter's moons, listed in the order of their orbits outward from the planet.

| MOON | | YEAR FOUND | DISCOVERER | DISTANCE FROM JUPITER, MILES | DIAMETER IN MILES |
|---|---|---|---|---|---|
| V | | 1892 | Barnard | 112,600 | 100 |
| I | (Io) | 1610 | Galileo | 261,800 | 2300 |
| II | (Europa) | 1610 | Galileo | 416,600 | 2000 |
| III | (Ganymede) | 1610 | Galileo | 664,200 | 3200 |
| IV | (Callisto) | 1610 | Galileo | 1,169,000 | 3200 |
| VI | | 1904 | Perrine | 7,114,000 | 100 |
| VII | | 1905 | Perrine | 7,292,000 | 40 |
| X | | 1938 | Nicholson | 7,350,000 | 15 |
| XI | | 1938 | Nicholson | 14,040,000 | 15 |
| VIII | | 1908 | Melotte | 14,600,000 | 40 |
| IX | | 1914 | Nicholson | 16,880,000 | 20 |
| XII | | 1951 | Nicholson | (Data not yet certain) | |

You can see that only the Jovian moons with names are really moons in the sense that ours is. The others are small enough to be captured planetoids, and may have been added one at a time to the original four.

All of Jupiter's small moons are probably captured asteroids. The true size of all such small moons is a little uncertain because of the distance and the difficulty of making precise measurements. They could be a mile or two either way. For that matter, some astronomers admit that we can't be certain of the precise distance of our own moon. There is a possibility of a few hundred miles error. But we're pretty certain of our moon's diameter.

Earth's satellite, with a diameter of 2160 miles, is only slightly larger than Europa and smaller than the other three major Jovian moons.

Ganymede and Callisto could, in theory, have atmospheres but none have been found. Io and Europa could have atmospheres of the heaviest gases, but it is unlikely.

Callisto does show one feature that is mysterious. It has a way of suddenly growing dark—not because sunlight is cut off, but because of some change that we cannot explain. It's as though the satellite suddenly started absorbing light instead of reflecting it. We may have to visit Callisto to find out the cause of this unusual, but infrequent, change.

Earth-type life seems improbable on the Jovian moons since there is no atmosphere, no water—unless there is ice—and temperatures over 200 below zero. Still, it is best not to rule out some form of life of which we know nothing.

Notice that Ganymede and Callisto are bigger than Mercury by about 200 miles diameter. The largest moon in the solar system, Titan, has a diameter more than 500 miles greater than that of our smallest planet. It is the only Saturnian moon larger than Jupiter's four. However, all of Saturn's moons have names, and it's possible that none are captured asteroids, with the exception of Themis, whose existence has never been proved.

*Outpost on Titan*

Dione, Rhea and Japetus are of respectable size, and Phoebe is a retrograde moon. But the star of the Saturnian system is Titan. It is the only moon in the system known to have an atmosphere. Unfortunately for our hopes of earth-type life, the air is not fit to breathe. It is methane, like Saturn's atmosphere.

| MOON | YEAR FOUND | DISCOVERER | DISTANCE FROM SATURN, MILES | DIAMETER IN MILES |
|---|---|---|---|---|
| Mimas | 1789 | Herschel | 115,000 | 375 |
| Enceladus | 1789 | Herschel | 148,000 | 450 |
| Tethys | 1684 | Cassini | 183,000 | 750 |
| Dione | 1684 | Cassini | 234,000 | 900 |
| Rhea | 1672 | Cassini | 327,000 | 1150 |
| Titan | 1655 | Huyghens | 759,000 | 3550 |
| Hyperion | 1848 | Bond | 920,000 | 300 |
| Japetus | 1671 | Cassini | 2,210,000 | 1000 |
| Phoebe | 1898 | Pickering | 8,035,000 | 200 |
| Themis | 1905 | Pickering | . . . . . . . | . . . . |

Beyond Saturn, no moons have atmospheres and all are far too cold for life such as we have on earth.

Notice that Miranda of Uranus was found in 1948 by Dr. Gerard Kuiper, almost 100 years after the discovery of Ariel and Umbriel by Lassell. The size of Miranda indicates that it may be a captured asteroid—except for the fact that none of the minor planets now have orbits that reach out that far. Of course no one knows how the asteroids were formed, although the most credited theory is that a planet broke up, probably because of the disturbing influence of Jupiter, and spread its pieces far and wide. Perhaps a few went far beyond Saturn's orbit and were captured by Uranus and Neptune. We may be able to tell better when we get there to see for ourselves.

Here are real facts about the moons of Uranus:

| MOON | YEAR FOUND | DISCOVERER | DISTANCE FROM URANUS, MILES | DIAM- ETER IN MILES |
|---|---|---|---|---|
| Miranda | 1948 | Kuiper | 81,000 | 150 |
| Ariel | 1851 | Lassell | 119,000 | 600 |
| Umbriel | 1851 | Lassell | 166,000 | 400 |
| Titania | 1787 | Herschel | 272,000 | 1000 |
| Oberon | 1787 | Herschel | 364,000 | 900 |

The Neptunian moon, Nereid, is one of the strangest in the solar system, but Triton is one of the largest. It is the size of Mercury. Like the smallest planet, it could have an atmosphere, in theory. No atmosphere has been found, however, and if Triton had one when newly born, it has since escaped into space or frozen into snow and ice. The temperature of Neptune is thought to be 330° below zero and that of Triton about the same.

Here are the real facts about Neptune's two moons:

| MOON | YEAR FOUND | DISCOVERER | DISTANCE FROM NEPTUNE, MILES | DIAMETER IN MILES |
|---|---|---|---|---|
| Triton | 1846 | Lassell | 220,000 | 3000 |
| Nereid | 1949 | Kuiper | 5,000,000 | 200 |

The possibility of frozen Pluto having a moon isn't completely denied by astronomers, nor is the possibility that there may be another planet beyond Pluto. There is no evidence for another planet except for odd movements by the outer planets as they travel in their orbits. One explanation for this behavior would be a tenth planet.

There are many things still to be discovered about our solar system, and a Plutonian moon and a tenth planet may be two of them.

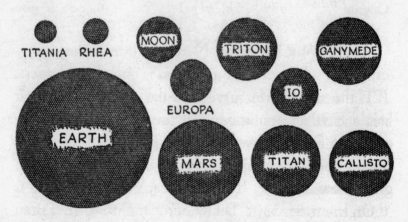

*The major moons compared with Earth and Mars*

# 17

# The Alien
# Space Ships

Ezekiel the prophet lived in the sixth century before Christ. This is the spiritual they sing about him:

*Ezekiel saw the wheel,*
*Way in the middle of the air.*
*Ezekiel saw the wheel,*
*Way in the middle of the air.*
*And the little wheel run by faith*
*And the big wheel run by the grace of God.*
*A wheel in a wheel. . . .*
*Way in the middle of the air.*

The story of Ezekiel can be explained easily. Symbols and allegories appear throughout the Scriptures, and Ezekiel's wheel was one of these. Or was it something else? Let's look at a few other wheels that may give us an idea.

On the morning of December 20, 1893, many persons in Virginia, North Carolina and South Carolina saw an object in the sky. It was luminous; the light was a brilliant white. The noise of it was heard. It passed overhead until it reached a point on the eastern horizon and stopped, remaining still for perhaps fifteen minutes. Then it disappeared. To some observers it looked like an enormous wheel!

This was 1893 and the first crude airplane was not flown successfully until ten years later, in 1903, by the Wright Brothers.

More recently, to take just one of the flying saucer reports, Captain Emil Smith was piloting a United Airlines plane on July 4, 1947, when he saw nine flying disks. They were in sight for about twelve minutes and were seen clearly enough by other members of the plane crew so that good descriptions could be given.

Wheels in the sky!

But how about "a wheel in a wheel," in the words of the spiritual? These have been seen, too.

There is a kind of aircraft design in which an outer ring whirls around an inner disk. It operates on the principle of the helicopter. The over-all shape is that of a saucer or a wheel.

The wheel seen by Ezekiel may have been just an allegory or a symbol, but it is curious how the words of the spiritual fit some cases where flying saucers have been seen.

Putting aside wheels for the moment, let's take a look at lights in the sky.

On October 5, 1877, the London *Times* reported a series of lights of various colors that moved over the

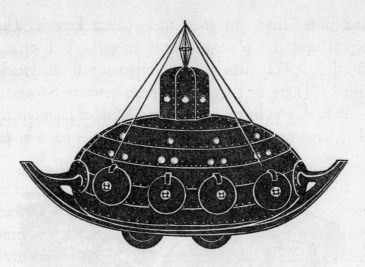

*Flying saucer—old version*

coast of Wales. This was before airplanes—and there were no balloons around Wales. There were about eight lights, traveling together.

On the evening of August 25, 1951, Dr. W. I. Robinson, Dr. A. G. Oberg and Professor W. L. Ducker, all of Texas Technological College, saw a number of lights race across the sky. The lights were in crescent formation and there were about thirty of them. A few minutes later another flight went across the sky. After that, hundreds of people saw the flights on various evenings.

A series of photographs were taken by an amateur photographer, Carl Hart, Jr. They show a number of lights arranged in formation.

The college professors agreed that they were not natural lights, but that they traveled without sound and faster than any man-made object known. The report and the photographs were published in the April 7, 1952, issue of *Life* Magazine in an article titled, "There is a Case for Interplanetary Saucers."

Wheels and lights are only two kinds of phenomena that have never been explained, and we have given

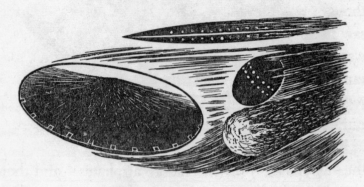

*Flying saucer—new version*

only four examples out of hundreds. There are also records of mysterious circular objects that hover above clouds, their light showing through. There are records of cigar-shaped craft. These records cover two centuries.

Here are two reports of cigars in the sky, one old and one new.

On the night of November 17, 1882, a cigar-shaped object passed over England. There can be no doubt of this. It was seen at the Greenwich Observatory and was described in the observatory publication. A report by another observer appeared in the *Philosophical* Magazine, and the London *Times* published letters about it. The strange object was surrounded by an aurora and it gave off a greenish light.

More recently, on July 23, 1948, Eastern Airlines pilots Clarence Chiles and John Whitted took off from Houston, Texas, on a night flight to Atlanta. Near Montgomery, Alabama, the pilots saw what they first thought was a jet plane. Then it came closer, and they saw it from about 700 feet away. It had no wings. It was about 100 feet long and cigar shaped. A blue glow ran the entire length of the thing. There were two rows of windows. It had what seemed to be a pilot compartment, brilliantly lighted.

There isn't room in this book—nor in five books of the same size—to report all the mysteries of strange objects in the sky. It has been the custom to laugh at strange reports and to say that the observers have been "seeing things."

They've been seeing things, no doubt about it. The mass of evidence is overwhelming.

The samples given for wheels in the sky, for flying lights and cigar-shaped craft are typical of both the old and the new reports. There really is nothing new about flying saucers or mysterious aircraft that fly without wings. People who have seen and reported them have been laughed at for at least two hundred years, and it is possible that a close look at folk tales and legends might show that the objects have been seen for many centuries. It makes you wonder. What kind of wheel did Ezekiel see?

Some of the reports can be discarded. Untrained observers saw natural things without knowing what they were. But time and time again, trained observers have seen objects for which there is no completely acceptable explanation.

There is always room for mistakes among human beings, but there is very little chance of a mistake in a whole series of "radar sightings." Radar is electronic. It reports only when there is something for the beam to strike. Radar beams can't strike hallucinations or "spots in front of the eyes." What's more, radar operators know the difference between a signal that bounces off metal and one that may hit a cloud. Flying saucers have been tracked by radar a number of times.

The Department of Defense and the armed forces have denied repeatedly that they are testing anything resembling flying saucers and cigar-shaped craft—except for the guided missiles program, which does not send rockets over cities on air lanes.

A remarkable man, Charles Fort, spent his life digging up such stories. He was laughed at during his lifetime because he had a lot of very odd ideas that were opposed to accepted scientific theories. Sometimes he said strange things like, "I think we're property." He meant that the people of earth are owned by unknown superior beings.

But Charles Fort didn't mean half the strange things he said, as anyone can see from reading his books. He had only one purpose, to poke fun at the kind of person who will not change his opinion, no matter what. This kind of person tries to explain everything in terms of his own theories, no matter how unsound the explanation may be.

Some scientists are guilty of this, and theories are sometimes developed which ignore the facts that don't fit. Fort's purpose in writing books was to give the public the facts this kind of science had ignored.

A great many of his reports were about strange objects in the sky. Time and time again he described things that we are wondering about today, like flying saucers, cigar-shaped ships, strange patterns in clouds, lights in the heavens and changes in the planets and on the moon.

Even if we throw out ninety-nine per cent of Fort's facts there is a pretty big number of reports in the remaining one per cent that just can't be put aside. The same is true of modern observations on sky objects.

Fort wrote four books which have been put into one volume called *The Books of Charles Fort*, published by Henry Holt and Company. No one who wants to think for himself and to make up his own mind about flying saucers can study the subject fully without reading Fort. Unfortunately, he had an odd writing style that does not make his books easy to read, but they are worth the trouble.

The article in *Life* Magazine is also important for those who want to learn for themselves about sky objects. Since most libraries have bound copies of magazines, the article shouldn't be hard to find. Another good article on the subject is in the January, 1950, issue of *True* Magazine.

The Air Force report on "Project Saucer" probably can't be found now, but the most important parts of it —including some pretty wild guesses about life on unknown planets outside the solar system—are quoted in Donald Keyhoe's book, *The Flying Saucers are Real*.

One conclusion we can draw from research on flying saucers is so serious that it is best to do some studying for yourself before believing it.

A large number of people, including some well-known specialists who are astronomers, physicists and engineers, have reached one conclusion about the sky objects. True, many others say that the conclusion is nonsense, but they have no really good explanation for the reports—except to say that they're not true.

*Life* Magazine answered these doubters when it said of the particular reports it chose for its article: "To doubt the observers in the foregoing cases is to doubt the ability of every human being to know a hawk from a handsaw."

The conclusion is this:

*Earth has been visited regularly for at least two centuries by space ships from another world.*

The reasons for this belief can be summed up as follows:

(1.) The speed of the mysterious objects and the way they maneuver. Any metals known on earth would melt from friction with the atmosphere at some speeds at which the saucers and the cigar-shaped objects have been clocked. Their high-speed maneuvers produce centrifugal force so many times greater than gravity that human beings could not live through it, no matter how well protected. The way the objects act has led trained observers—like Air Force and air line pilots—to say definitely that they are piloted and not remote-controlled.

(2.) They seem to have engines better than anything of which our engineers have ever dreamed. These power plants are silent; they give no evidence of an exhaust or moving parts and they are capable of tremendous accelerations. They have enough power to hold a battleship motionless in the air with no sign of a jet, a propeller blade or anything else. Some of the saucers and rocket craft have been as big as battleships. It is certain that the power does not come from chemical reaction, like our engines. It is almost equally sure, for good, scientific reasons, that the power does not come from atomic energy. It is possible that these alien spacemen know a way to use the gravitational fields of planets and stars for power sources.

(3.) The saucer—or disk—is a design that will work in air, although not very efficiently. Disks wobble when whirled through the air at high speeds. Some of the flying saucers have been seen to wobble. But the disk is probably the most practical design there is for a space ship, once space is reached.

These are good reasons but they raise a big question: If it is true that we are being visited by alien spacemen, why haven't they landed and tried to contact us?

We don't know. It's possible that the spacemen are so unlike us that there is no way to communicate. It's possible that they're taking time to learn all about us before they try to make contact.

It's also possible that they are just keeping an eye on us to see if we're about to become dangerous.

Such spacemen would have a more advanced civilization than our own. Their mysterious power plants show that. They might be so far ahead of us that we are considered primitive creatures who should be watched. After all, since the first recorded reports of unknown sky objects almost two hundred years ago, the world has gone through one war after another, each one worse than the last.

Now we have atomic energy. An advanced civilization on another planet would be able to see and identify our atomic test bursts—and Russia's. The latest mass of flying saucers arrived soon after the first atomic bomb was set off in New Mexico.

We're getting ready for space travel now, and perhaps the peaceful beings of another world are a little worried about having warlike earthmen drop in on them.

But this is all guesswork. We don't really know. We don't really know that the flying saucers are space ships. However, only the alien space ship theory so far gives a logical answer to the behavior of objects which very definitely have been seen, measured and tracked on instruments and by airplanes.

It's best to make up your own mind by reading everything you can find on the subject. The list of books in the Appendix should be helpful.

Another question is, if we are visited by alien spacemen, where do they come from? Again we could only guess. But instead of listing guesses we can list some puzzling mysteries that may give you an idea.

Mars is the planet most people think of immediately. It comes the closest of any planet in the solar system—with the possible exception of Venus—to having conditions under which earth-type beings can live.

Callisto is another interesting world. We have mentioned that Callisto has a way of turning black for no reason that we can find. But this Jovian moon isn't the only thing that turns black. Certain places on our own moon do, too. The crater Plato is the best example. Plato sometimes turns dark at high noon, when the sun is shining right into the crater. The darkness can't be explained by shadows.

In 1870 there was a very strange series of lights in

Plato. In one night three astronomers recorded lights which, they said, could not have been sunlight. The lights seemed to be in a pattern and the number varied from four to twenty-eight.

Plato is not the only moon crater which has shown such changes, but it has shown them more often and more dramatically.

And there is the crater Linné, which has changed from light to dark and back again and which has shown changes in its shape.

We mustn't overlook Venus. Charles Fort records several periods when flying saucers became numerous while Venus was closest to earth.

Alien spacemen might come from outside the solar system, too. We don't know how fast their ships can go. They may be able to reach the speed of light or even pass it, although this is hard to imagine.

Some astronomers have tried to estimate how many planets there may be in the universe and how many might support life. We would be able to make a better guess if we knew more about how life began.

The universe is a tremendous place, with so many billions of suns that it is very hard even to understand the meaning of the number. There may be a hundred million planets which have life of some kind on them. There may be many more than that. We must remember that our sun is not the grandest kind of star and that our planet isn't very much of a world even in our own solar system. The same forces of nature that created life on earth must have acted on other worlds, too.

Out in the unimaginably vast reaches of space there must be worlds with beings more intelligent and advanced than we, and worlds with people more primitive than we. If we accept this we must also accept that

*Other worlds around a distant star*

some of the advanced people have already traveled through space.

We use the word "people," but it is unlikely that the beings of other worlds look like Terrestrials. The laws of chance, however, would allow a possibility that beings from worlds the same size as ours—and with the same atmospheres—might be like us.

Science fiction writers have been suggesting for years that spacemen might already have walked the earth. There have been stories in which leprechauns and pixies turned out to be beings from other worlds.

Science fiction has value. One purpose of this book

is to help separate present possibilities from future ones. It is also to help you know when a television program or a story is based on sound science. Good science fiction never takes more than limited poetic license with sound science. Writers like Heinlein and Bradbury use present-day knowledge as a springboard to the future.

It isn't beyond possibility that someone reading this book may become a physicist—and someday apply Einstein's Unified Field Theory to an idea he once read in a science fiction story, thus giving earth the kind of power drive the flying saucers may have.

It could happen. Once you get interested in space, the sky is no longer the limit. The only limit is the end of the endless universe.

# 18

# Outward to the Stars

Space travel. Interplanetary flight. Interstellar flight. Intergalactic flight.

These are dreams, but at least space travel and interplanetary flight are dreams that can come true. For the others, flight to the stars and other galaxies, we'll just have to wait and see what the years bring.

A few years ago, the idea of firing artificial moons into orbits around earth would have seemed like a fantastic, impossible idea. But, if you're lucky, you may see these man-made moons for yourself.

Launching the first satellites is only the beginning. Other, bigger ones will follow. We don't yet know when, but we can be sure it won't be long. Then will come the day when man himself follows his rocket trail into space.

The first satellites will tell us a great deal about the problems of getting men into space. But they will do more than that—they will also solve some big legal problems. For instance, how far upward does a nation's territory extend?

The first satellites will decide whether American rockets can travel high above Russia's skies, and whether Russian rockets can travel over our own land. Fortunately, the satellite launchings have no military purpose. They are being launched only for reasons of science, and scientists of all nations have been invited to cooperate.

The American scientists are working together under the United States National Committee for the International Geophysical Year, and this committee is operated by The National Academy of Science. Our committee is working with the national committees of other countries through an organization called the International Council of Scientific Unions.

Our committee hopes that scientists of other nations will help to track the satellites once they are launched. This will be a difficult job because the satellites will be so small. Amateur astronomers have been asked to cooperate in keeping track of the tiny moons.

At certain times, when your part of the earth is in shadow right after dark but the satellite is still in the sunshine high overhead, you may be able to see one. The newspapers, and publications like the *Sky Reporter*, which may be obtained from the Hayden Planetarium in New York, will carry exact information to help you locate one of the tiny moons.

If one of the satellites should fall to earth at a time and place that made it possible for you to watch, you could see it clearly as a great meteor. Of course this would be pretty much a matter of luck. But who knows? You might be one of the lucky ones.

After Project Vanguard is at an end, some time will go by before the next launchings. Probably these will be unmanned satellites, too. But each launching of an unmanned rocket takes us closer to the day when the first spacemen will seal rocket ports and speed to space.

The first manned trips will not be smooth ones. We will fumble, make mistakes, and learn as we go. Brave men will pay with their lives for the opening of the great frontier. Space will not be bought cheaply.

For those young people who are truly interested in space travel, and who want to play a part in the wonderful and exciting events of the coming years, the time to start preparing is now. All sorts of special skills and talents will be needed. In fact, they are needed right now.

Here are just a few of the specialties that space travel needs: Engineers of several kinds, electronics experts, chemists, physicists, communications experts, doctors, metallurgists, experts in ceramics, experts in celestial mechanics. And if atomic energy should be used, reactor technologists, heat exchange experts, health physicists and a number of others will be needed.

The only sure way to play a part in the coming age of space travel is to have a skill that space travel needs, and such skills take education and experience.

*Spacemen in the uniform of tomorrow*

Meanwhile, keep up with the news of space travel. But think about what you read, and what you see on TV. A great deal of nonsense already has been written about space travel, and there will surely be much more. If you think about what you read or see you will be able to tell which is sense and which is nonsense.

Of course this is true of everything, not just space travel. It applies to what you read about atomic energy, or flying saucers, or new discoveries on other worlds.

No one can truly foresee the future, and it is very hard to make any kind of prediction about space travel. So much depends on what we expect from space travel, for instance. The first satellite launchings are for scientific purposes, and there would surely be more scientific information to be gained from any space projects. But the cost is very great, and it may be that the future of space travel will depend on its military value.

Many things have been written about how important space stations would be to our Armed Forces, but it is unlikely that some of the ideas are very practical, while others may make the cost worth while.

One thing, however, seems to be sure, and that is that progress is hard to stop. The launching of tiny, unmanned satellites surely is not the end. In some fashion, exploration of space will continue. Only time can give us details of future developments.

There may even come a time when space travel will be taken for granted, as air travel is now. Fifty years ago, there was as much excitement over the first flights of aircraft as there is now about the sending of rockets into space.

It doesn't seem likely that trips to other planets will become commonplace within the lifetime of any persons living today, but who knows? Scientific and technical developments are coming so fast that it is impossible to keep up with all of them. Perhaps the science of space travel will progress more rapidly than anyone now guesses.

Meanwhile, we can keep our eyes on the skies. Man always has looked upward to the stars, and perhaps that is where his ultimate destiny will be found—on far-off worlds that today are only twinkling points of light in the awful immensity of space.

# Reading for Rocketeers

In the following selection, an attempt has been made to describe the books briefly according to subject and reading difficulty. They represent only a small fraction of the books available. Your bookstore or library can help you find others.

CHESLEY BONESTELL and WILLY LEY, *The Conquest of Space*. (The Viking Press)

Bonestell's color paintings of other planets are not only wonderful to see, they're as accurate as present knowledge can make them. Willy Ley's text is clear and interesting, and contains one of the best sections on asteroids yet published. Good reading for all ages, although young readers may have to study a bit.

ARTHUR C. CLARKE, *Exploration of Space*. (Harper)

The most recent book by this author. Somewhat less technical and perhaps even more interesting than *Interplanetary Flight*.

ARTHUR C. CLARKE, *Interplanetary Flight*. (Harper)

One of the best books written to date on the "how" of space travel. Mr. Clarke, an official of the British Interplanetary Society, gives the mathematical basis of interplanetary flight as well as a clear description of some of the problems that will be encountered. The mathematics may be difficult, but young readers will get quite a lot from the book anyway.

JACK COGGINS and FLETCHER PRATT, *Rockets, Jets, Guided Missiles and Space Ships*. (Random House)

For younger readers. A simple description of how rockets work, with a brief but good history of rockets.

CHARLES FORT, *The Books of Charles Fort*. (Omnibus edition, Henry Holt)

These are remarkable books. Not easy reading, even for adults. Take in small doses. The sheer mass of Fort's information will convince you that there is much we don't know about our own world—much less other planets.

KENNETH HEUER, *Men of Other Planets*. (Pellegrini & Cudahy)

Here's a delightful book the whole family will enjoy. Heuer pays little attention to the "how" of getting to space, but goes into excellent detail on what we may find.

JOHN LEWELLEN, *You and Space Travel*. (Children's Press)

For young readers. Mostly about the theory of flight, with a good description of how jet planes and rockets work.

WILLY LEY, *Rockets, Missiles and Space Travel*. (Viking)

The most complete work of its kind. Detailed history of rockets from earliest days. Excellent bibliography. Not easy reading because of the mass of detail, but worth the effort.

JOHN P. MARBARGER, ed., *Space Medicine*. (University of Illinois Press)

The first collection in book form of scientific papers on human factors in space flight. It is authentic and important. Probably too technical for young readers.

HAROLD LELAND GOODWIN, *The Science Book of Space Travel*. (Pocket Books and Franklin Watts, Inc.)

A book for adult readers by the author of "The Real Book of Space Travel." A detailed explanation of the physics, engineering and general background of space flight.

# Index

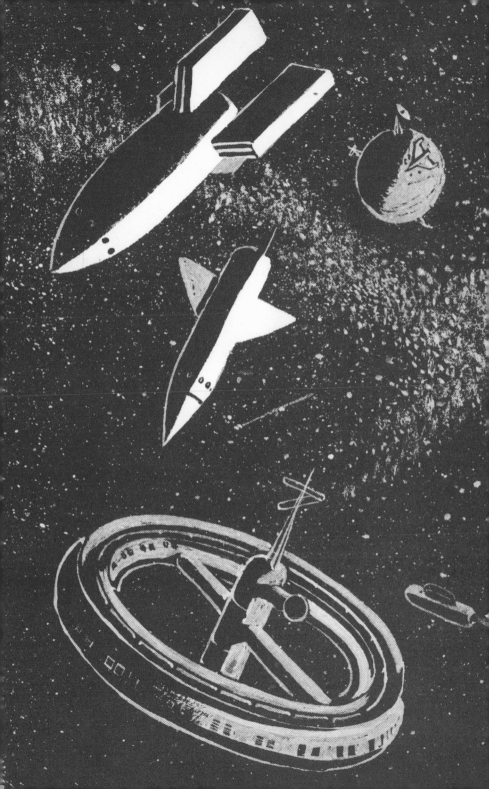